RESTLESS HEARTS

WHAT IF FALLEN HEROES
COULD GO HOME?

DENNIS O. BAKER

abbott press®

A DIVISION OF WRITER'S DIGEST

Abbott Press books may be ordered through booksellers or by contacting:

Abbott Press
1663 Liberty Drive
Bloomington, IN 47403
www.abbottpress.com
Phone: 1-866-697-5310

Because of the dynamic nature of the Internet, any web addresses or links contained in this book may have changed since publication and may no longer be valid. The views expressed in this work are solely those of the author and do not necessarily reflect the views of the publisher, and the publisher hereby disclaims any responsibility for them.

Any people depicted in stock imagery provided by Thinkstock are models, and such images are being used for illustrative purposes only. Certain stock imagery © Thinkstock.

ISBN: 978-1-4582-1193-4 (sc)
ISBN: 978-1-4582-1192-7 (hc)
ISBN: 978-1-4582-1191-0 (e)

Library of Congress Control Number: 2013918172

Printed in the United States of America.

Abbott Press rev. date: 10/15/2013

Epigraph

Heroes never die. They live on forever in the hearts and minds of those who would follow in their footsteps.
—Emily Potter

Dedication

Dedicated to all the service men and women who have served their country honorably, gifting their country with the sacrifice and bravery that only disciplined and impassioned warriors can understand.

United States Army
United States Navy
United States Marines
United States Air Force
United States Coast Guard
National Guard

INTRODUCTION

Restless Hearts is a fictional novel that honors all military, including active duty, reserve, and veteran servicemen and servicewomen. This is a tale of hope and destiny. The book is intended to evoke the thoughts of the reader to examine what possibilities exist, and the resultant heartache when there are abrupt endings to life.

The individual stories introduce five servicemen and showcase their lives on the day before each one leaves for war. Enter a young man who has reservations about choices that he has made in his life. As the story proceeds, he is mentored by those who never had a second chance. This book takes the reader into a fantasy of second chances for the characters and unveils the secret, heartwarming truth behind a hidden facet of the main character's life. In the pages of Restless Hearts, you will discover that those who have the least in life sometimes have the greatest gifts to give to others.

This story shows that there is a place in everyone's life for new beginnings, or at least gives readers pause and makes them think about their own lives and their personal impact on others who make up the circles of their lives. If life ended today, would your influence leave a positive, lasting footprint in the world of your loved ones?

ALONE

B uck sat on the bench under a sign that read, "Saint Mary's Catholic Boys Orphanage." It was an ivy-covered stone building that stood a couple of blocks away from Main Street. He was tossing pebbles into a puddle that had appeared early that morning from the hard rain the night before. Buck would close his eyes and dream of a better life far away from New Orleans. He was thin, quiet, and except for infrequent celebratory moments when new children would arrive, he stayed preoccupied in his dream of the future. His clothes were tattered and unwashed. His hair was thick and cut in a bowl-like fashion.

It was common knowledge that most of the children who arrived at the Ninth Ward Orphanage came from the ladies of the evening. The ladies would become pregnant by visiting sailors or affluent cheating husbands, but when they either couldn't afford, or for reasons of influence, did not want to raise their little prizes born out of the lusty, whiskey soaked nights. So the orphanage with the hard-working women of religion would bear down to provide basic survival needs to these little less-fortunates.

Each ripple in the rain puddle carried him like a ship to distant oceans and for the adventure for which he so yearned. He had lived his fourteen years at Saint Mary's, with the ever-revolving carousel of transient brothers and guardians. This particular morning would be life-changing, though, and would take him away to places never dreamed. His home reference was a run-down shanty crowded with sibling tenants. He had recently become increasingly nervous that his day of exodus would be imminent because past experience was that the older boys left to make way for new additions.

Buck wasn't like the others. He thought about who his parents might be and how he would find them someday. He longed to be loved by someone and hoped to find a family, and an order of existence that was difficult for most during the onset of World War I. He ached for the next chapter in his life, yet he was fearful at the same time.

The heavy wooden door of the orphanage behind him creaked open. A bulky figure donning a habit stepped through. Buck looked up, and his lip began to quiver. He sensed that the time for change was here and all that remained were the spoken words. Although he had been abandoned before, this would be the time that he would feel it to his core. The seeming contradiction for him now was that he was ready for change but so afraid to go forward. Mother Rosalie stretched her winged arms toward Buck. He hesitated, thinking that if he didn't touch her, her message wouldn't penetrate his being. He reacted slowly with the hope that the words would never come; anything to prolong his stay in what had served him his entire life.

Mother Rosalie gave her normal spirited salutation.

"Good morning, Buck. Are you ready to go?"

Buck tried to smile, hoping for a new life and new opportunities, but deep within he owned an overpowering feeling of being lost again and starting all over.

She smiled as she sat beside him on the bench.

"We'll miss your help with the younger children. You have been with us for near on fourteen years."

Buck only knew the orphanage as his family. He had been abandoned as a baby, and, since his earliest recollection, had seen a revolving door of transiting, unconnected characters.

Mother Rosalie smiled, and then with her pudgy digits gestured to him for a hug.

Trembling deeply, he tearfully responded. "Please let me stay. I'll Do Anything You Want."

She quickly rebuffed. "Buck, you have to start a life of your own. You'll meet new people and learn to make choices that will change your life. You'll see many years of happiness and prosperity. God will watch over you."

Buck stood hopelessly, wiping his tears with his ragged sleeves.

Rosalie chirped again. "It wouldn't be fair to turn another away to make space for you, Son. Now, please get going before the storm comes again. Here is two dollars to get you through the next week."

He turned and walked down the street in the direction of the train station under a darkening sky. He still didn't fully comprehend that this evening he would be alone, no shelter, no food except the few pieces of bread that he had stuffed in his pockets while the others weren't looking. He wasn't far from the train station and would make his arrival there in about thirty minutes if he picked up the pace. He felt a couple of raindrops and began running to find the closest cover.

The gloominess of the day reflected his sad state of mind. His melancholy spirit was a great beginning reference, he thought, because he knew that his life could only get better. He didn't wallow in self-pity or wonder about the prospects that might become him because he had never had this freedom of feeling before. The choices that followed wouldn't be based on any experience he had known. His ignorance put him at an incredible disadvantage, and he only hoped that the world would be kind.

As Buck got closer to the train station, he marveled at the masses of men gathering. He wondered where they were all going. Mothers hugged their young sons, while young ladies kissed their husbands goodbye. Sadly, many of them would never be seen or heard from again. The conductor began to corral the young men onto the train as the outstretched arms were ripped from their loved ones. Buck wasn't sure where they were going, but he saw that they resembled him. They seemed to be going through the same process that he had experienced earlier with Mother Rosalie.

He walked out from behind the tree and headed for the train, blending in with the sea of those heading out. So, without any hesitation, he ran to catch the last open door. It all happened so quickly that he didn't think of where he was going or why. As the train departed, fathers and brothers cheered them off to war. The lost faces filled the windows as they pulled away on their journey to find their place in history. Buck sat alone, head down, and never looked back.

ANCHORS AWEIGH

Chief Petty Officer Charlie Koberlein rested against the corner of the garage waiting for the charcoal to turn white. He pulled a pack of Chesterfields from his cuffed cotton t-shirt, tapping a cigarette out the end into his nicotine-stained fingers. As he lit the end, his mother and sister, Helen, walked out the back door carrying corn on the cob, baked beans, and rolls.

That evening in Chicago was incredibly gorgeous. Charlie threw the hamburgers and hot dogs on the grill. The smoke billowed, and he jumped back. Helen giggled.

Just then, his dad pulled up into the driveway with a six pack of Schaefer next to him on the seat. He leaned out of his truck window, smiling.

"You'd think that a big bad Chief could handle a simple grill. It'll be much easier handling the beach in Hawaii and sailing around the South Pacific."

Charlie hollered toward the house. "C'mon Granny, we don't have all night!"

His mom stood at the screen door wagging her finger. "I'll give you granny, young man. You're not that big that I won't put you over my knee."

They sat and ate quietly as the evening sunset colored the table. Charlie broke the silence. "It'll be hell for those Japs when we steam that way. We'll kick ass and then take names." His mom imparted one of her famous looks of disapproval and then looked away with sadness in her eyes. Then the discussion began on world events and what the future would bring.

Helen spoke up. "I wish they'd stop all the fighting and bring those boys home."

Charlie returned with his tough guy response. "The *Arizona* will sink everything in her sights. We'll make history!"

His father began scolding him. "Charlie, knock it off."

Mrs. Koberlein stood up and began picking up the plates, but Charlie pleaded. "Mom, Helen and I will get it. Go relax and we'll be in soon."

He took the plates from her hands, set them on the table, and apologetically hugged her.

"I'm sorry, Mom. I'll be okay, and we'll be home before you know it."

SILHOUETTES

A young, spirited couple sat at the table in the corner of a smoky, old juke joint in Vernon, Texas. Their silhouettes were colorfully projected on the wall by way of the lights of the jukebox animation. Tony Burr was leaning into his girl, Ruth, as they listened to a barely audible Jane Froman's "I'll Walk Alone."

Young Tony tried to brave the remainder of the evening with smiles and kisses while the love of his life mimicked his resolve. She was that gorgeous, wholesome girl that every mother wanted her son to bring home. Ruth was impassioned with her soldier-to-be.

As they sat blindfolded to what life had prepared for them, their romance brewed greater with every passing moment. They ignored the dangers that would mark their path. They couldn't have picked a worse time to live and love than in 1944. It would only be a couple more hours of gazing into each other's eyes and then one last romp literally in the hay. They had planned the next part of their evening where the farmer at the edge of town would be quietly tucked in his home, and the animals soundly stalled. It would be then that they would perfect their love one more time.

Tony looked at his watch and smiled big. Ruth batted her eyes, blushed, and looked away with all the innocence that came easily her way. In truth, though, her feelings were more like, "Let's get it on!" They practically ran out of the honky-tonk, slipping through the trees and side streets, evading the view of any spies in the night. It took five long minutes before they ended up at the entrance of the barn. Tony scanned the street to see if anyone had caught their movement, and within seconds they were through the door, laughing and grabbing each other. They stopped only to see the big brown eyes of the cattle noting their every move.

Ruth anxiously reached up, smiling in anticipation for Tony to pull her dress up over her head. Tony accommodated her lead and in one fell swoop had her down to panties and bra. Tony reached up into the rafters and grabbed a blanket that they had planted on a prior soiree. Ruth hated the prickly straw sticking her in the backside. Tony normally obliged his girl taking bottom to absorb the pain.

They shared an incredible passion for each other; one that most couples dream of. Tony's departure would be a new experience for them. They were childhood sweethearts and had never endured separation, but for the time left, they had agreed they would not talk about or think about the next morning. Tony and Ruth normally stayed out late so their parents would be asleep when they returned. On this night, though, they would stay gone all evening.

As they lay there in the night, they couldn't help but think about and talk about the future. After all, what is life without the dreams of a new day? Ruth insisted that regardless of the outcome, she would be right there waiting. Tony reassured her that there was no need for worry.

Ruth held Tony's chin. "I just can't stand it."

Tony lay there silent. Inside, it was like he knew that the future would take them on a path which wouldn't return them to the place from whence they had come.

Again Ruth expressed her concern. "Tony, what if?"

"Ruth, I don't know. I do know that we are strong enough to beat anything that this world has to throw at us. You know we have always been there for each other. Our relationship is built on a true love with heaps of trust on top."

Her look of terror, and the tears that slid down her cheek, prompted Tony.

"Ruthie, let's not talk about it anymore."

"I'll be waiting here for you, Tony, always."

The two stretched their arms around each other in a deep embrace, passionately kissing, and beginning their next and final act of love. There was not time for sleeping that evening. The animals grew restless, which was their signal of pre-dawn. Ruth got up while Tony lay there. He had to have one last look-see of her delicious outline presented against a background of stars shining through the boarded cracks.

"We'd better skedaddle before we get found out."

"I don't really care, Ruthie. When I get back, we'll have a house of our own and can sleep together. You can bring me breakfast in bed and then we can play all day long. Then I'll make dinner and serve you. A little dancing in the parlor and life will be so grand."

He hesitated and then followed. "But, if I don't get back . . ."

Ruth touched his lips. "Shhh."

Tony grabbed her arms and began. "Ruthie, please promise me that if I don't come back, you will go on and live a happy life. It's all I will ever ask of you. It's what I want."

Before she had a chance to respond, he opened up the barn door and looked out. They snuck back to their homes undetected.

Tony planned to meet Ruth at her parents' home at 8:00 a.m. Shortly after Tony arrived home, his mother summoned him to the kitchen for a hearty breakfast. She hoped it would hold him over for the long bus ride. While his mother made conversation, he was preoccupied with leaving Ruth. Tony's father came in from the barn and sat down for the last meal with his son. He had noticed a blanket in the hay but didn't speak of it to Tony.

"Son, I think Mom has outdone herself this morning on the chipped beef on toast. Of course it will look, taste, and be called something entirely different in the mess hall."

Mrs. Burr was pleased to see her son devour her cooking but knew that it would be his last good meal for a while. Tony stopped shoveling it in just long enough to wash it down with a cold glass of milk. They could tell that he was preoccupied, and they never gained his complete attention.

Finally, he came back to the conversation. "I guess it'll take a few days to get to base. I hope that we get this over with in short order."

"We just hope that you make it there and back safely. Your father and I will be checking the mail every day, so please write."

Her voice cracked and tears welled in her eyes. Tony got up immediately to comfort her. She felt that this was the time in life when she could no longer protect him from the struggles or dangers that life would be serving up. This was the first time that his father couldn't provide relief to his mother.

"Mom, Dad, I'll be fine. You taught me how to take care of myself. I promise to come back in time to take in the hay next summer. Besides, I can't keep Miss Ruthie waiting too long because she might find another man. That can't happen."

His mother responded with a smile. "That little lady won't even look at another boy. She'll be here whenever you return."

"I don't think that I would want her to do that Mom. That wouldn't be fair if I never came home."

His mother's finger drew quickly in his direction and wagged. "Don't you."

"I'm sorry. I will be home sooner than you know."

Tony angled in for one of his famous mother-son hugs and extended his hand to his father.

"I've got to be going. I'm meeting Ruthie at her house, and then we're heading to the bus station. I've got to be there by noon."

His father looked at his pocket watch. "That's three hours from now."

"I know," he responded with a sheepish grin.

They stood silent for a moment, and then his parents reached out their hands for family prayer. They bowed their heads while Tony read their faces with his eyes affixed to their expressions. He realized that they had never faced this kind of pain before. He captured this in his memory. It would serve as incentive for him to come home safely. He was struck by the power of the moment, the eloquence of his father's words, words that he had never heard from his father's heart before. He sensed the hope and prayer through his dad's tightly clenched hands and trembling voice. It was as if death was imminent, and this was a step in the process of acceptance.

"God, we ask that you provide safe passage for our son and bring him back to his loving family to live a long and prosperous life. Amen."

Tony hugged them both again, reassuring them of his safe return.

"I've got to go. I'll write as soon as I get to my unit and know where we are going."

His mother's voice trembled. "We love you, Son. Be careful. We'll be sure to have Ruthie over from time to time for dinner."

"Thanks, Mom."

He headed for the door and turned to wave goodbye. He wondered if he would ever see them again but quickly changed his thoughts to Ruth. He realized that saying goodbye to her would be tough. His heart was hurting from the pain he had seen in his parents' eyes, yet he was smiling with the hope of a lifetime with Ruthie. He ran the gambit of many emotions.

Ruth was waiting impatiently on her porch in her granny's rocker. The staves creaked against the planking at an increasing pace as the minutes ticked away. In the distance she saw his lanky frame making its way down the street. He had dark, wavy hair combed back with the front pulled in the shape what was known as a duck's ass. His front teeth slightly protruded, but to her it made him special and one of a kind with his own special smile. Everything about him was icing on her cake. At the very mention of his name, she beamed, eyes sparkled, and she'd be a giggly mess.

In his mind, Tony kept a permanent photo of Ruthie, sitting on her porch. She kept her blonde hair neat, in a page boy, and her brown eyes were as deep as a well and full of radiance. Her full figure drove him crazy just like the early pin-ups of the war, except this one was his. Her smile could only be outdone by her dimples. She loved life, she loved him, and as the livestock could attest, she loved him good.

Tony called to Ruth. "Hey lady, want to go on a trip to a foreign country with this lonely soldier?"

"Can you, will you take me? Don't tease me."

"I would if I could, Sweetie. Can you fit in my duffle bag?"

"If I weren't so big."

"I love you just the way you are."

"Tony, my folks wanted to say goodbye."

"Okay, but make it quick. I want to spend every moment with just you."

Tony rushed through the farewells, and then he and his Ruthie scurried off to be alone. They spent the next twenty minutes walking along the street, with arms around each other's waists, in total disregard to the traffic and onlookers. They didn't care. Nothing else existed in their world for the moment. As they got closer to the bus station, they found a bench in front of the soda fountain.

"Would you like a soda?"

"No, thank you."

"Ruth, I want to make sure that you are okay while I'm gone."

"I'll be fine. I'll miss you terribly, but I'll be right here waiting for you."

"I don't want you to wait if I don't come back."

"Tony, please quit saying that. I hate the thought of your not returning."

"Well, if I don't . . ."

"Stop it."

He pleaded with her. "Please let me say this once, and I won't say it again. If I don't come home, I want you to find a life for yourself, even if it means finding someone else to make you happy."

It killed him to say that. He couldn't stand the thought of anyone being near his Ruthie.

"Tony, I won't. Listen closely; I won't ever be with anyone else. I don't care what you say. It's what I want."

Although he was relieved to hear those words, he still loved her enough to truly want her to be happy, even with somebody else.

"I love you, Ruth. I want to have a long life with you, with children, and a big house, and maybe a little barn in the back for us to roll in the hay."

Ruth blushed, and smiled big. "Yes, that would be wonderful."

They sat quietly, wondering what would really become of them. Time passed quickly, and soon the bus appeared in the distance. They stood up and embraced. The bus pulled to the front of the station, and the door opened. The station manager told them that the bus would be picking up and then leaving immediately. Tony held Ruth close as he kissed her passionately.

The driver cleared his throat to signal Tony to board. He threw his bag over his shoulder and held on to her until the last possible moment. Tony leaped onto the stairs with the door closing directly behind him as he rushed to the back of the bus to wave goodbye. Each of them wondered when they would be together again as they watched each other's shadows become dots. What would become of them? The last image in Tony's mind was of Ruth stepping into the street pointing at the ground.

His memory was of her looking down and mouthing words that would remain in his memory. "I'll be right here waiting for you, Tony."

TROUBLED MAN

Major Ricky Wood was hypnotized by the sights and sounds of war blaring from his Magnavox television. It was 1968, with no end in sight for the flyboys. He was oblivious to his two children, Jimmy and Lesa, playing by his feet. They were close by him for the evening, knowing that he would be departing in the morning for Vietnam. Each one hoped to win a moment's worth of his attention. They sensed a pain in him that was evident by his sharp, curt words. Ricky flew F-4 Phantoms for the Air Force and had on occasion buzzed the house on weekends while the kids were playing with their friends. Jimmy and Lesa were proud of that daddy, but now they knew a different man. That night they saw a man that they hoped would leave so that their other daddy would return.

Betty Wood stood in her kitchen in Malmstrom Air Force Housing watching her children beg for their father's attention. She had hoped that he could at least muster up enough decency to hold his children, talk to them, or even acknowledge their existence. Instead, he was zoned into ABC Nightly News with propaganda from the front, and not making heads nor tails of what was next, besides the heartache of war.

Perhaps his unhappiness stemmed from the uncertainty of his future. However, he never conveyed his thoughts to his wife or kids. His actions were gruff and short with no apology to follow. He was consumed by it all. He couldn't distinguish his home front from the warfront.

Betty tried to recall better times of a husband who used to project joy each time that he would come home. She leaned against the doorway and closed her eyes. She was sad for him and the kids one moment, and then she would get pissed. In frustration, she turned to the reefer to grab another beer to put his sorry ass to sleep. Then she would know just a little peace in her heart.

Knowing that he was leaving in the morning, she just couldn't bring herself to argue and complicate the evening for the children. There were times when she would think about a life if he didn't return, then become remorseful. She leaned across his chair to switch out one can for another and regretfully kissed him on the cheek as if to apologize.

Ricky was surprised. "Betty, I'm trying to watch."

She retreated to the doorway again and began to strategize how she would get the kids a proper goodbye from him before going upstairs to bed. Betty was painfully aware that fathers don't always come home, and she never wanted to regret not making this right for the children. He wasn't making it easy for her to do her job as the military wife.

"Okay kids, kiss Daddy goodnight, and get to bed. It's going to be an early morning."

Each grabbed a knee and hopped up for their gratuitous kiss before heading off.

Lesa whispered in her father's ear. "Daddy, I love you. Can we go with you in the morning to the hangar?"

"No, Baby. I have to leave long before you get up."

He hugged his little renegade tightly for a moment and kissed her on the cheek, looking over her shoulder at the television not to miss one fascinating piece of the report. Lesa looked at her mom for a smile of reassurance that he would miss her. Jimmy tried to get eye to eye contact to have Rick's undivided attention, and then he hugged him and jumped off to go upstairs.

Jimmy smiled. "I'll write to you, Daddy."

As the distractions walked away, Rick thought for a moment that maybe he was missing something. Then he turned back to the news. Ricky couldn't help being consumed by something more important than his family. It was his job to teach his family to be tough and fend for themselves because that's how it would be when he was gone. He could never figure out why he would be a bastard at home, and then while he was gone he wanted to make it right. He just couldn't seem to get it straight.

After they had all left the room, he relented. "Why should I put up with this? Maybe I won't come back. They wouldn't miss me anyway. I'm better off dropping napalm and following it into hell."

Betty flipped the bathroom switch, straightened the rug, and headed to Jimmy's room. She wanted to quell any unwanted thoughts that he may have, and to reassure him that his dad truly loved him.

"Jimmy, did you brush your tooth?" He always laughed at that line. Betty had been a Dental Hygienist for a short period before she got married. She was always a champ at taking a bitter pill and changing it to sugar for the children.

Jimmy asked. "Why is Daddy mad?"

"He's not, Honey. He has a lot on his mind with leaving, and it hurts him to have to be away from us."

"Does Dad have to fight in the war?"

Betty could lie straight-faced for the children's sake. "No, he doesn't, but he will be gone for a few months helping others to be safe. Then, they can go home to their families just like Daddy will come home to us."

"Why can't we go and watch him fly away tomorrow?"

Again Betty minimized. "It's too early, and he knows that it will not be good for you to be sleepy in school."

Betty combed her fingers through his hair and smiled, hoping that he wouldn't ask any more questions.

"Go to sleep and save your questions for class. That's what Daddy would want you to do."

"I love you Mom, and I pray that Daddy gets back in a hurry so that we can go fishing at Canyon Ferry."

In past years, Ricky had taken the family to Canyon Ferry fishing and camping. Those were much better times, when Rick would pick up Jimmy and Lesa on his shoulders so that they could dive into the water. Betty would stand watch to secure the boat while Ricky and the kids enjoyed the day without a care in the world.

Betty hungered for those days when they were happy. She wondered whether it was her or the war. She hoped that it wasn't his family that had drained his energy and his character. She tried her best to make him smile, regardless of her own private moods of regret, or struggles as a military wife.

Before long, Jimmy had fallen asleep, and then it was off to see Lesa. She took a couple minutes to compose herself, and then passed through the doorway. Lesa held her arms behind her head and smiled. Lesa seemed to understand the situation and served as a comfort to her mom during trying times.

"Well my little angel." That was all she could get out before Lesa interrupted her.

"Mom, why can't we live with Grandpa and Grandma? Then Dad wouldn't leave us all the time. Aren't you afraid that one day he won't come back?"

Betty tried to collect her thoughts quickly, with an answer that would suit Lesa; however, her daughter seemed to be reading her mind. That question had been tormenting her for a decade. The truth was that it had only been within Ricky's last deployment that her fears had grown. At times she felt self-centered in regard to her feeling that it would be easier alone, without him, though it might bring greater happiness to her children. It wouldn't be fair to leave him, because she knew that this was when he needed them most.

She took a deep breath, and then began to explain. "Honey, your dad has trained for this job since he finished college. It would be selfish for us to take that all away from him. He is the best fighter pilot in the world. It's something that he dreamed about for the entire time that we dated through high school."

For all the gobbledygook that Betty had just imposed on Lesa, it seemed that she wouldn't ask again, but kids sometimes sense what may be real versus fantasy.

"But Mom, don't people want to do what makes them happy. Daddy doesn't seem to be happy any more. I'm afraid that he might not come back from the war."

Betty brushed her daughter's hair away from her eyes and smiled, still trying to provide a reasonable response that would stop the inquisition.

She began pouring her heart out before she realized that it was too much for Lesa to consume. "Lesa, I have known your daddy since I was a little bit older than what you are now. He is a determined man who wants the best for his family. He's going through a rough patch with so much on his mind. The best that we can do for him is to try to understand and hope that he comes back to us in the way that we want him to. I pray every day that he will be happy, and that we can all laugh and play as we once did at Canyon Ferry. There isn't much else I can say."

She abruptly left this discussion for a later time, years down the road when things would either change, or Lesa would grow to understand as a woman. Betty held Lesa tightly for a minute and then kissed her on the forehead.

"Good night, Sweetie."

"I love you, Mom."

Before Betty made her exit, Lesa shot back again. "Please don't be sad. You have us, Mom."

Betty felt guilty as hell for her openness. She went back to hug Lesa, but it was more to console herself.

"I love you so much. It helps me more than you know that I have you here to help me. I'm sure that you will be my strength for many years."

Betty stood up again, tucked the blankets under Lesa's body like a sleeping bag. She grinned, held back the tears, turned and walked out closing the door behind her. She stopped by her bedroom to turn down the bed for her and Rick and she lit a candle by the bedside for their last night before his deployment. After setting the stage for romance, she sat on the edge of their bed, knowing that any sexual advances would go unanswered. She picked herself up and bravely walked back down the stairs to face the lover that she had once known.

As she hit the bottom step, she could see her knight in shining armor dreaming of a better life.

"Ricky, are you ready to go to bed?"

She tapped him on the shoulder hoping not to startle him. "The kids are asleep, so I thought that we would do a little 'get-ahead' before you leave in the morning."

"I'm tired. You'll have to take a rain check."

She had come to know that as his parting line for any occasion. Sometimes she would think to herself that one day he would want her, and she might have the same comeback. "Yeah, how about those apples pal?" she whispered under her breath.

Being the good wife and trooper, she smiled, hoping that she would at least get a cuddle or maybe a chance spoon in the night. Those advances would be her own.

Ricky sat up on his throne, gathered his surroundings, and launched to the stairs. Betty quickly secured the television and lights, and followed closely behind. She hoped that they could talk before he drifted off. Rick lifted the sheets, slid under, and turned his back to her, while she climbed in on her side.

"How about a kiss, Honey?"

Ricky craned his neck and offered an air kiss. "I'm sorry. I'm so tired."

She cautiously asked. "Ricky?"

His raspy voice responded. "What?"

Betty hesitated for a minute to make sure she couched her words to his favor. What she wanted to say and what came out were two entirely different thoughts.

"Please be careful. The kids and I are worried. Lesa's words were that of a grown little girl, and Jimmy, all he wanted was his old dad back to go fishing with him."

She waited patiently for his response. The next sound she heard was that of wheezing as he had already fallen asleep.

She spoke lowly, hoping that he would hear her words. "I love you, too, Rick. Please come back the way you once were. I miss you terribly, even though you're right here."

She rolled back the other way and snuffed out the candle. For a time she wrestled with her feelings, and then her love came through. She turned to his back and snuggled close, placing her arm around his waist. Unconsciously, he grabbed her hand. They were down for the count until the alarm sounded at 3:45a.m . . .

"I can't believe it's already morning. Betty, did you pack my stuff last night?"

Rising with his voice, she responded like his next in charge.

"Yes, Dear. I packed everything you asked for, and a little more."

Betty would always put treats and notes from the kids in his flight bag. She never forgot to stuff a love letter from her to him on all trips. And she had a little brown stuffed monkey that traveled with Ricky anywhere he went. He would always smile whenever he unpacked and found the little guy. The romance in her heart had never faded, and her hopes were that each return would rekindle the fire and happiness in their hearts. She couldn't quit the ritual that had been so instrumental in their love life.

"Thank you."

Ricky walked to the bathroom, closing the door behind him. There used to be a time that he would dance to the "rain locker" while his young wife would watch in delight as he performed for her in the shower. Betty dragged his flight bag down the stairs because it was too heavy to carry. She lugged it to the front door and set it down.

While Ricky finished getting ready, she kept busy in the kitchen, pouring a glass of orange juice and making a bacon and egg sandwich on toast with a swipe of ketchup on one side and butter on the other. She turned the radio on to keep her company, but mostly to take her mind off of his departure and her impending loneliness. With one click, the local DJ announced the Four Tops with a fitting melody "Ask the Lonely." She placed his brown bag breakfast on the corner of the table and plopped down to listen to the sad words—

> "Just ask the lonely
> they know the hurt and pain
> of losing a love
> you never can regain"

Betty felt that the lyrics fit her in her present state of mind. She wondered whether she had lost the fire, or was it that with every match she struck, Ricky's emotional absence would suck the oxygen from the air to snuff it out. And the second verse added to her isolation—

> "But ask the lonely
> how vainly a heart can yearn
> for losing a love
> that will never return"

Ricky walked into the room and interrupted Betty's daydream. For a moment, she had escaped into her world of hope and pity. She didn't know which she preferred at this point. She remembered a time when they had danced to life and filled the house with music, love, and laughter. Her days had become more about thinking, now. She recalled a "Love Is" poster that Ricky had purchased when they first met. It had served them well for so many years. It read-"Life is a tragedy to those who think and a comedy to those who feel."

Ricky tried to gain her attention. "Betty, I need to get going."

"Ricky, I asked Candice to look in on the kids and told her that I'd be back in an hour."

They walked to the door, Ricky picking up his bag. It was becoming increasingly difficult for Betty to continue trying. She was afraid that when she tried to rise above and show affection, Ricky would play it off and reject her. She was thankful that the kids weren't there to see that. The trip to the flight line was short and quiet. The guard saluted as they approached the security gate.

"You can just let me off in front of Ops."

"I'd really like to see you off at the tarmac, Rick."

"I'll be fine. Then you won't have to fight the traffic or people and can get back to the kids."

Betty wanted this last opportunity to bring some emotion out of the old bastard. She was becoming a little peeved with his indifference. She was willing to try, so why wasn't he? She didn't want to press her luck and anger him in front of his troops, nor did she want the public display of non-affection.

"Okay, Rick."

She was thinking to herself that it would be more difficult to maneuver in and around the people to drop him off rather than finding a spot in the parking lot. Was he that miserable that he couldn't spend the next hour with her before he went to brief his flight? She had all but given up the ghost. She finally found an empty Duty Driver's spot next to the entrance. Quickly, she took it. Ricky got out, put on his cover and took his bag from the back seat. Betty got out and met him at the front of the car.

"I love you, Rick."

"I love you too, Baby."

"Rick, please take care of you. I hope this is the last trip that you make. I feel that every time you go, we lose a little more."

"Betty, what are you talking about?"

"I want to go back to us again. I want the life that we once knew. What happened?"

"Betty, this isn't the time."

"I guess not. Just come back in one piece and get this nasty war out of your system. I just want all of you. I think that this is sucking the life out of you. I know it's killing us."

Ricky looked at her somewhat puzzled, but deep inside he knew that he was unhappy with it all. He wondered how it had happened, why it had happened, and how he could have distanced himself from the very things that meant the world to him. He couldn't face her honestly because he couldn't figure it out on his own. The duty driver showed up for his spot so they each hugged again and he turned to go.

"Please take care, Ricky. I love you."

She didn't know if he heard her words. She had that feeling of talking to herself again. Another deployment, and another long, lonely time alone.

Afternoon Delight

Army Sergeant Allan Milk was a fun loving, regular guy, a country boy from the Catskill Mountains. He'd been earning extra credits at his folks' dairy farm while on leave from Iraq. He wanted to put the war behind him. This was a dream come true. It's what he had thought about night after night while lying in his rack after dry, dusty days of chasing bad guys and out-maneuvering the IEDs.

She was a spectacular, pony-tailed blonde who made Daisy Dukes look delicious regardless of fray. Her name was Donna, and she was his bride of three years. The noise of the John Deere 40 and baler made it hard for any conversation, but they didn't care.

They were just elated to be together. Donna sat on the wheel fender in all her sexiness. Allan kept his hand on her slender, athletic legs. He would swear that he was only tending to her safety without any ulterior motive. She would argue that he was a horn dog taking any liberties with her that would gain him a roll in the hay. After all, what good is making hay without making hay? Their foreplay consisted of longing smiles, winks, and a wagging tongue.

They dropped two wagons of hay at the barn for the cousins to offload. It was all part of a bigger plan. In all his wisdom, Allan knew that would keep them busy at the barn while he and Donna settled into the last long row around the field. As they neared the backwoods, he stopped the tractor, turned on the tractor radio, and grabbed a blanket from the baler twine compartment.

"What do you have on your mind, fella?"

"Hold on there, little lady. I'm setting the mood."

"You mean, you need a mood for this?"

"Afternoon Delight" began to play, bringing a wide smile to her face. It was that provocative smile that always drove him nuts.

She became concerned. "Allan, they'll think we're having problems with the equipment."

"Isn't a problem with this equipment, Baby."

He quickly began undoing his belt. Without hesitation, she submitted to his advances. She knew if she delayed that there would be more chance of getting caught in the act.

"Go for it tiger."

Allan didn't need a second invitation. They were so used to enjoying each other, as if it were still their lustful, teenage years. Donna looked deeply into Allan's eyes.

"I wish this would never end, Al."

He grabbed her firm ass, pulling her close.

"Allan."

"Hey, shhhh, I'm trying to get something done here. No speaking please."

She wrapped her legs around his and pulled him in close. They probably wouldn't have been able to hear anyone approaching, being consumed with each other. He immediately rolled over to allow her the control and comfort of top. They were tightly entangled for about ten minutes and then lay on the grass in the shade of, and looking up at the big pine tree.

"Is it always going to be like this, Allan?"

"Like what?"

"You know, always saying goodbye."

"Just think, every time I get back, its honeymoon all over again. How great is that?"

"I know, but what happens if you don't come back?"

"Won't happen. Besides, I'm not a lifer. I want to come back and run this farm. It'll be great, sexing you all the time in the field, in the hayloft, on the kitchen table. Want me to go on?"

"We'd better get back at it again before they come checking on us."

With that, Allan gazed at her thighs.

"Yep, would like to get back at that."

"C'mon Al."

Donna became a little irritated trying to get Allan to be serious about their future. He was leaving in two days, and she knew that there wasn't a lot of time to talk about their future. However, she also knew that he looked to her for her carefree and lighthearted approach to life. She wanted more explanation, but just didn't have the heart to corner him on this glorious day.

Allan didn't have patience for serious talk, especially around his family. Inside he was eaten up by the war, but his façade told a much different story. They remained quiet all the way back to the barn. He would think about the future on his next deployment. It seemed like a vicious cycle. When he was gone, he would make promises about the future, and when he was home, he would forget what he wanted to change about their life. He'd rather focus on play time with Donna than be serious about future, real life plans. His philosophy was living in the present and enjoying everything that life had to offer at that moment.

They rounded the sheds on the tractor, toward the unload crew. The workers smirked and waved. They knew what Allan and Donna had been up to, and Allan returned his huge smile as if to say, "Guilty."

BEACH BABY

Like all Navy Seals, Frankie was in his element at Dam Neck Beach, but more specifically, on this day his mission was with his family. Lieutenant Leonardo epitomized the Seal persona as dashing and muscular with an overflowing cup of charisma. Today he was teaching his three-year-old recruit, Austin, survival techniques in the chilly waters of the Atlantic Ocean.

Sara, the very curvaceous, beautiful brunette, and patient wife of Frankie, was settled up under her umbrella, reading a romance novel. Occasionally, she would glance over her book to observe her big kid, Frankie, and her little kid, Austin, playing in the sand. She would chuckle inside, thinking that her bigger kid was more of a handful.

"Frankie, let Austin use his own imagination."

"Just trying to get it right so the bad guys can't break through."

She grinned big. "I'm sure. He's just a boy, as are you. Don't you think we should go? It's cooling off, and I don't want him to catch a chill."

With a wink and a smile Frankie fired back. "Yes, we do have to conduct some sheet operations before I leave tomorrow."

Frankie scooped Austin into his arms and headed to the water. Sara heard a blood-curdling scream as they hit the water.

"Frankie, it's cold!"

"Sara, I've got to get the sand off. Besides, I don't want him to grow up to be a pussy."

"Time to go and you know that I hate that word."

They gathered their gear and headed toward the parking lot. As soon as Sara was in striking distance, she dope-slapped Frankie. He unsuccessfully tried to outmaneuver her hand.

"Now who's the wimp?"

The trip home was filled with silence. Each was reluctant to face the next morning with words. Instead, they stowed the beach gear, toted the little sleeping recruit to bed, and worked steadily to complete the chores in preparation for departure day. Sara went upstairs and lay across the bed watching her sailor stuffing his duffel bag with more clothes than it would hold.

"How do you do that?"

"Do what?"

"Get so much in that bag."

"It's all in the folding my dear."

"I guess."

He stuffed the last webbed belt into the duffel bag while Sara began stripping for the shower. Frankie lay across the bed at this point, propped up his chin and asked, "Mind if I watch?"

"Well sailor, you can help me get some of the sand out of the hard to reach places."

She didn't have to offer twice. Before she could close the shower door he had his clothes off with soap in hand.

"Okay, start at my shoulders and work your way down."

"I think I've got this well under control, Missy."

"Oh, that's right. It's the Marines that I have to give instructions to."

"Real funny, Sara."

He began to lather the washcloth, and then proceeded as instructed.

"Yes, right there."

"I was thinking lower."

"Now, do it right, Frankie."

"Circles, I think circles. Relax your shoulders and go with the flow, Sweetheart. Daddy's in control now."

As he moved down her back with the cloth, he reached around to lather her breasts.

"And you are breaking your move on me now?"

"Shhhhh. Go with it."

She was standing in front of him now leaning against the glass. He steadily migrated south to the Promised Land. She would always drive him wild when she puffed her sweet round cheeks against his groin. Then it was Katy bar the door after that. Neither could stand it. They stayed in the shower until the water began to cool. They rinsed, dried, and retreated to the bed. It wasn't long before the two engaged their bodies again with Sara in control. It was understood in their marriage, there may not be a tomorrow.

The mantra of the warriors who are always on the edge of death missions is normally live life to the fullest. That mantra in this case would be demonstrating his intense love for his wife. Then, there would never be any regrets of ever having fallen short. They would collapse in each other's arms, exhausted from the intensity of giving themselves, to an afterglow that would remain until the next time.

After a while, she rolled to her side. He cozied up behind her in a spooning fashion with his arm around her.

"What time are you leaving?"

"About zero dark thirty."

"That tells me a lot. He began to touch her again, wanting more. Is that all you think about? You know that I get antsy every time you go, especially on your secret squirrel trips."

"Sara, I am one well-trained machine. I'll always be back here for you and the maggot."

"Why would you pick the most dangerous job in the world? It would be nice to have a semi-normal life with you. It gets hard with just Austin."

"See, you're never alone."

"Funny . . . You know what I mean. You get to run off everywhere and travel. Well, you know. You're always busy and don't have time to miss us."

He pulled her toward him, and she cried.

"I miss you guys every day. I can't imagine hurting you or not being here. We have our whole lives ahead of us. I love you more than you can imagine. You and Austin make my life what it is."

"Then promise you will come back in one piece, please?"

"I promise."

He got up to turn off the bathroom light and then opened the shades to let the moonlight shine on their naked bodies. They held each other tightly and eventually drifted off to sleep.

CHOICES

Pete Baker was hard headed most of the time, to the point of his pain. His friends would tell him that he would rather be stupid than wrong. On this particular night, Pete, an intensely principled young man, would argue his motives again, much to the chagrin of his parents. His parents, Kent and Arlene, stood in one corner of the kitchen desperately debating the seriousness and complexity of choices that Pete felt were quite simple and honorable for any spirited, red-blooded American.

Pete exclaimed, "I'm telling you that I want to make a difference! I want to be someone! Every able-bodied American should serve his country. It's what America is all about."

"Son, you haven't thought this through and should consider how these thoughts and actions affect your mother."

"Dad, so many of my friends have already signed up and left."

Arlene walked toward Pete in a begging fashion.

"Pete, you would do so much better if you went to college first. You were accepted at William and Mary and have a very bright future, much more than the other boys who don't have that opportunity."

"Mom, I don't care about college right now. Hell, I don't even know what I want to be when I grow up."

"You'll be so much more after you have finished college, and you would be able to be a commissioned officer. That would mean more pay, more responsibility, and a better future once you got out."

"I may never get out. Besides, how do you know so much about the ladder of success in the military? You and Dad just don't know. You haven't been there."

Kent replied. "Your mom has a better idea than you think, Son."

Pete got riled. "Oh really?"

Arlene chimed in. "Pete, I didn't raise you to go off to war and get killed."

"You make me sound like a goofball who can't get out of his own way. I have a good head on my shoulders and can take care of myself."

"But you never know what can happen. Your chances of survival in today's style of warfare present a rather big challenge to anyone. You could be so much."

Pete settled into the argument. "I really think that I will be more out there changing the world than sitting in a classroom, hiding behind a desk."

"You really should listen to her, Pete. Your mom is smarter than you think and . . ."

Kent looked to Arlene to finish the conversation with a nod and an intense look of surrender.

Arlene continued Kent's thought. "I have had a lot of friends in the area who saw their husbands off to war when you and I were much younger. It was pretty horrible watching their entire lives changed when the CACO showed up at the door."

Pete looked at her inquisitively, wondering what a CACO was. Arlene turned her head slightly away to hide the tears. Pete didn't understand her emotion, and at this point didn't want to discuss it any further.

"We've had this talk too many times. If I went to college, it would be a waste of your money. My heart would be thousands of miles away fighting a war that my body would be absent for."

His feelings were difficult to dispute. The room fell quiet as they broke from dialogue to exchange looks. With one last volley, Arlene led into the next discussion.

"Look at all those poor young boys and girls going over there now and coming back disfigured either their bodies and/or their minds. I couldn't bear that thought for you. They haven't made much change for the nation, yet it changed their lives forever."

"That's a pretty shitty thing to say, Mom. They have done more than those who never wore a uniform."

"You're just too emotional, Pete."

"Pete, why don't you at least try one semester before you decide? That's a fair request from your mom and me."

"I would have thought you would know who I am. You raised me."

Pete walked out, slamming the screen door so hard that a hurricane lamp on the porch table fell and shattered.

"Pete, come back please."

"Sorry, Mom. I'm outta here."

THE LONG WAY HOME

P ete had survived the past few years after walking out on his parents and enduring the intensity of Navy SEAL training. He was never prepared for the turmoil that had filled his life within the last few days and the last thing that he wanted to face was additional turbulence. About one hour after takeoff over the Atlantic, the C-17 Plane Commander announced that the flight would be bumpy for most of the next ten hours. Pete brushed it off as part of the piled-on-mess that he had been served in the last week. He couldn't remember much of last week, except that he had watched his best friend and shipmate, Lieutenant Frank "Frankie" Leonardo, take a bullet to the back as he signaled for his group to move forward on point.

It was all one big nightmare. Pete was there to catch Frankie before he hit the ground. Or, was it that Pete wanted to believe that he was there to catch him? He walked over to Frankie's flag-draped transfer case to secure the tie downs for the impending movement. He walked all the way around the case to make double sure that everything was in order, still not believing that all this was actually happening.

Pete wouldn't have let anyone else serve as escort even though he had no idea what he would say to Frankie's wife, son, and parents, or if he could hold it together in public. Frankie's flag-draped transfer case sat in the back of the aircraft among four others that were geometrically placed about the pallets in a military fashion. Red nightlights provided sufficient illumination to remind the passengers and escorts that they were not alone. Pete moved about to hide in the shadows and to hide his tears for the fallen. He was thankful for the roar of the engines that masked his occasional sobs.

As he leaned against the fuselage next to Frankie's body, he began what he thought would be a final one-sided dialogue with his friend.

"I guess there comes a time when a man should take inventory of how he lived his life, loved his family, and served his country. How many lives are attached to one fallen soldier? What happens to those left behind? I guess when it's all said and done, those who died gave up any chance of ever being there for them again. I never gave much thought to what was involved in a relationship, and just how special it could be. I sold my folks out in my self-glory for country. They didn't deserve what I did to them."

Pete walked around to the other side, between the transfer case and the fuselage. He placed his trembling hand on the container just like it was his Bible and began to swear this solemn oath.

"Damn, I just lost my closest friend. I'll remember you till the day that I join you. I promise you, Frankie that I will embrace every moment of love, whether it is from my folks, my friends, or a new girl. There are no moments left for you, Buddy, but I promise from this day forward that I will soothe the many restless hearts that I know are still out there."

Pete stopped for a moment for another announcement of turbulence. Then, he continued his talk with Frankie. "How in the hell do I look your family in the eye? I swore to your folks and Sara that I would be coming home with you. She's going to be so pissed at me, and you, too, you dumb ass. You gave up a pretty sweet gig for this station in life. You're a hero, but how does that work for them?"

Another escort surprised Pete with a tap on the shoulder.

"Hey Bro, first time?"

Pete tapped the case. "That should be me in there. I don't know what I can say to his family."

"It'll come to you. It always does. Like magic, the words will flow if you believe in your journey."

"I hope so."

"You do need to get your act together before we land."

He walked away leaving Pete behind to deal with his torment. Pete uttered a bromide, feeling sorry for himself.

"I can't believe this. This sucks. I'd change places in a New York minute. No girlfriend, no kids, no parents. I might as well be an orphan. Hell, Mom and Dad don't even know that I'm coming home."

With that, Pete walked to his seat and slumped down, covering his face with his jacket, and, exhausted from the emotion, quickly fell off into a deep sleep.

SOME LIKE IT HOT

P ete dozed off and began dreaming of better days.

In his dream, Pete and Frankie were spending the afternoon running together during BUDS training at Coronado Beach, CA. They were always competitive, each wanting to outdo the other for bragging rights. Luckily, their talents were equal in the physical training realm, keeping the kinship unparalleled to most. They were amazed that they had made it through hell week without much ado and that they were coming into their own in terms of their acceptance into the coveted Navy SEAL family.

Frankie was always the lucky one at love, though, keeping Pete in the corner to watch from afar. Pete respected the relationship that Frankie had with Sara, and to that point they had always welcomed him into their family circle. He had gotten to enjoy the family without the physical comfort of a bedmate. Sara's considerate nature had never made Pete feel like a third wheel. Many times he would sit and watch Sara and Austin interact, and think that it used to be that way with his own mother. He hungered for the relationship again with his own family whenever he hung with the Leonardo's.

Frankie was gaining on Pete as they turned the last corner to the barracks. This time Pete would slow to give his friend a positive stroke that would lead into the night that lay ahead.

"Well Frankie, you win. And I guess you'll win again tonight when Sara makes it to town."

"You betcha, Shipmate."

"And you'll be staying in that fancy schmancy Hotel Del Coronado. I would have loved to have been alive when Norma Jeane stayed there. I would have snuck into her room for a romp."

"Who the hell is Norma Jeane?"

"Marilyn Monroe. I've been in love with her since forever. Did you see Michelle Williams play her in "My Week with Marilyn?" We're talking hot, hot, hot, enough to, you know . . .'"

"Who hasn't?"

"Maybe you can get Sara to bleach her hair. She's pretty hot, but I think that as a blonde . . . and on the beach . . . with her body . . ."

"Eat your heart out, asshole."

"I'd love to have what you've got, Frankie."

"Yeah, she's pretty sweet."

"Yup. I'd have to stay at the Navy Lodge on my pay. The Coronado has some pretty steep fare, but I guess for a Lieutenant, it's chump change."

Frankie winked. "They're worth it. I'll get up with you later, after check in. See you in the lobby around eight?"

"Okay. Hey . . . wait. You pick them up at three, and you won't be in the lobby till eight?"

Frankie sheepishly smiled heading out of the shower in the buff. He took delight in saying that she'd be spanking this tonight as he pointed to his posterior.

The evening sun was setting deep in the west, creating a small cast shadow of Austin shoveling sand in his bucket. A few feet away, Frankie and Sara laughed, sipped scotch, and listened to a cover band play Adele's "Rolling in the Deep." The simulated lights of the evening from the patio began to dance all around the table creating an ambiance of chillaxing and relishing the tranquility of the present.

Pete strolled up sporting his congratulatory grin. "I see you guys made it early."

Frankie answered. "The little one woke up and wanted to play in the sand."

Sara jumped to hug Pete and planted a big kiss on his waiting lips.

Pete looked at Frankie. "Maybe you should leave us two alone?"

Frankie rocketed back. "Fat chance, Romeo. That's the closest you'll get to getting laid tonight."

"Frankie, you don't know what you have here."

"Wanna bet?"

Sara piped up. "Okay boys, there are little ears picking up every word you say."

They all settled into their seats and chatted up the day's events and what tomorrow would bring.

NIGHT MOVES

The Plane Commander was announcing on the intercom that everyone was to buckle up due to extreme turbulence. Pete woke up groggy and found he was extremely nervous about seeing Frankie's family. He was feeling caged and unable to take action on his feelings. He continued to fixate on the case. Unwilling to just sit there, he got up and snuck over to get comfort from his friend. He knelt next to Frankie's case, out of sight of the others.

Again he sought solace through Frankie's spirit.

"Frankie, how did we get here? You gave your life for some freakin extremist. You promised them a forever. Who'll play catch with Austin? Who'll romance your lady now? I bet it'll be some guy smart enough to stay home. They were treasures that you, my friend, can no longer enjoy. Frankie, I would give my life so that they could have your life back. If only . . ."

A deafening alarm filled the aircraft bay. Red lights flashed quickly and further confused Pete's state of mind. He reeled from a violent aircraft yaw, heard a couple of explosions, and then lost view of the case. And within seconds, the aircraft violently slammed Pete against the fuselage and then back toward Frankie's case, hitting his head. He fell to the floor between the case and the bulkhead, and it was lights out for Pete.

He couldn't ascertain how long he had been out, but the darkness that had surrounded him began to get light. Struggling to get to his feet, he fell from fuselage to case and back again. He was checking himself for injuries and the extent of the damage. He couldn't see any blood and noted nothing out of the ordinary. Pete quickly walked around Frankie's case to check the security. He noticed that all the escorts and passengers were sitting quietly in their seats, neatly tucked away and resting. He looked over to see the crew chief standing there.

With all his focus and force he blurted out, "Hey Chief, what the hell just happened?"

"What's up?"

"The explosion, the lights, the alarm?"

"A nightmare, I'm sure."

"Bullshit."

"Whatever."

"Hey Pete . . ."

Pete spun on his heels and didn't believe what he was hearing. He couldn't believe his own eyes. He rubbed them, shook his head, and opened them big again.

"Frankie?"

"You're looking at him."

"I don't understand."

"You wanted answers, Shipmate. So . . ."

"This isn't happening."

Pete walked away and sat in a seat well away from the rest of the others to collect his thoughts. He normally remained cognizant of his surroundings when in chaos. It's what Navy SEALS learn from the very first day of training. SEALS have to be in step, and on top of every scenario. He kept walking circles as if one foot were screwed to the floor.

He attributed the current situation to intense emotions and lack of sleep during the last couple of weeks.

He talked to himself. "What the hell is happening?"

There was nowhere to run to, or anyone to go to. His best friend and fellow SEAL was in a box and unavailable for consultation. Or was he?

"Pete, howgozit?"

Once again he saw a shadow that resembled Frankie but passed it off as being groggy or maybe a hard hit to the head. Pete looked for a place to sit away from the others. He covered his face with his hands and took the crash position. Could this be the end of his life? Was it that he saw Frankie instead of the white light that the spiritualists talk about? There was so much that he hadn't done in his life, and now it was ending.

Pete had maintained throughout most of his life that he wouldn't have regrets of any kind. There was that one sticky unfinished drama with his parents. Of all his cocksure boldness as an elite warrior, he found himself a little more humble now at what might be his end of life. He thought that it was too late to fix it now. An overwhelming feeling of remorse settled in his conscience.

Frankie stood smiling, while Pete wrestled with himself in the seat.

Frankie shook his head. "Whatcha got going in that head of yours, Buddy?"

Pete wasn't about to submit to what he thought now were his final moments. He lifted his head slightly and cut his eyes around the plane to get a grip on his surroundings, strategizing his next move. He noticed that the others were either sleeping or calmly chatting. How could they be so relaxed during this? He bowed his head and closed his eyes, trying to remove himself from the present. All the while, he tried to ignore his dead friend, or the likeness of him standing before him.

Being a hard-headed warrior, he usually accepted only those things that were living, breathing, and in-your-face real. Pete had offered the sale of his soul to return his dead friend back to his family. So, was this the deal coming to realization? Pete had requested fantasy, and here it was. The angst of having to report Frankie's death to the family should have now subsided.

Then regret poured back into the mix. So, what was he hoping for? Perhaps an opportunity to right misgivings, or a cowardly exit from life to join his friend? The longer his self-struggle ensued, the deeper he found himself bartering with whatever he thought might cut a deal.

Again Frankie asked, "Pete, what are you doing?"

Pete fired back. "Quiet!"

Pete wasn't about to let anyone or anything influence his tactical escape from the present. This consequence was his to own, and he wasn't going to let go of what he thought was his last speck of sanity. He was on the brink of screaming, hoping to summon a reaction that would make this real. He felt his motion, his eyes were open, and Frankie was talking at him?

Frankie faced Pete directly. "Well?"

Then he sat down in the next seat and leaned toward Pete.

"Pete, stop for a minute and talk to me."

Pete stared, waiting for the next words to form.

He intently watched Frankie's lips purse as he began to speak. "We need to talk about the next few days, Pete."

Pete was captivated with each word and sound that spilled from Frankie's dead body. He knew that this body was lifeless not more than ten minutes ago and now he was rambling like a Chatty Kathy doll. Pete reached over to touch Frankie's lips like a drunk would do to shush another.

Frankie pushed his hand away. "C'mon Pete, cut the crap."

Pete smiled. "Okay, whatever you want."

"Pete, we'll be landing in thirty minutes, and you need to have your shit all in one sock and tied at the end."

Pete fired back sarcastically. "You can count on me, Frankie."

Pete was toying with Frankie at this point just for reaction, but mostly to assess what the hell was going on. He kept looking around to see what the others on the plane were doing. He thought he had gone mad with all the pressure and pain; thinking that there would possibly be white jackets to greet him on the tarmac in Dover. He continued to ignore Frankie's insistence to engage in a discussion. When Frankie would start to speak, Pete would look away.

Frankie moved a little closer to enhance dialogue with Pete. "You didn't think that I considered what would happen to those I left behind?"

Pete responded. "You left them. What are they going to do now?"

"Pete, we knew the risks. Sara and I talked about the what-if's many times."

Pete looked at him in disgust. "And how does that make it better?"

"Pete, they will always love me. I know that, and that they will forgive me."

Pete couldn't believe that he was receiving counseling from a ghost, but he continued. "I thought that they would miss you when they aren't having such good times, the really tough times when they would most need your strength as a father and a husband. Frankie, was it really worth it for your country?"

Frankie explained. "It only matters that following us will be those who really care about their country and the generations to follow. That we made it a better place, a safer place for our spouses, children, and others important to them."

Pete chuckled. "I think you're in fantasyland, my friend, which fits this discussion, since you aren't really here."

Frankie argued. "Pete, have you given up so easily? I never would have thought that you would lose faith so easily. I have a little journey that I want to take you on to learn the truth. We'll see how others feel about what they have done for family and country. I think that when you see the cost of life for each of them, and the peace in their hearts today, you may come away with a better idea of what being a warrior means. You certainly could have made better choices in life, especially at home."

"What's wrong with my life?"

"Your pissed off attitude towards your folks."

"They didn't understand."

"Maybe it's you, Pete. Perhaps you never took the time to ask the right questions."

Pete shook his head like he was trying to wake up. He gave up the ghost and pulled his jacket over his head to sleep.

RESURRECTION

The C-17 Plane Commander's announcement blared their final approach to Andrews Air Force Base. Pete pulled his jacket down and looked to his left, and then right, to see Frankie sitting there. It was driving Pete insane that this dream wasn't ending. Still in disbelief, he sat quietly, beginning to feel a peaceful resolve come over him. By the time the aircraft touched down, he had become resolute that he'd just go along with this farce, whether it was real or not. His curiosity morphed into a serene level of acceptance, waiting to see what might happen next.

Pete would steal glances toward Frankie. He couldn't silence his SEAL-learned intuition of analyzing unfamiliar situations.

Frankie realized this and stifled Pete's eager unspoken inquisitions. "Would you just chill?"

"Easy for you to say, Frankie. You have nothing to lose."

Frankie smiled. "Touché, Matey."

Pete's ADHD kicked in. "So, what's next?"

The aircraft taxied to spot, the wheels were chocked, and the engines began to wind down as everyone began collecting his gear. Pete was calculating Frankie's every move to determine how he would follow.

"Where to, Frankie boy?"

Frankie gestured for Pete to follow. "We've got lots to do, and little time."

They exited the plane and headed toward Andrews Base Operations. They filed past the Petty Officer of the Watch and to the last door on the right, which housed the Duty Driver. Inside the office, Petty Officer Wax was sitting on his bunk eating chips and watching television. Frankie knocked on the half-opened door.

Petty Officer Wax asked, "Can I help you, Lieutenant?"

Frankie answered. "Yes, we need a ride to Arlington Cemetery."

The driver looked puzzled that they would want a ride at this time of night to Arlington.

"Sir, aren't they closed?"

The creative SEAL barked back, "We have a classified meeting tonight!"

The driver knew better than to question the Lieutenant and began putting on his boondockers.

"I'll be with you in a second, Sir."

"Thank you."

The driver exited the office and walked down the passageway to alert the Petty Officer of the Watch of his assignment. Pete, Frankie, and the driver loaded up in the van and headed west, toward Arlington. This was the first time in two months that Pete and Frankie had been in the U.S. They sat quietly thinking about their last liberty together in Coronado. Those had been much better times. It was the last semblance of sanity that the two had shared before running through the mountains of Afghanistan. The moon, however, was hanging high in the sky just like it had a few nights earlier when Frankie had lost his life.

SPIRITS

The Duty Driver drove slowly toward the entrance of Arlington Cemetery. The moon illuminated the gates in the fashion of daylight. The driver was unsure what beckoned the Lieutenant and Petty Officer to this solemn site at such a late hour. He curiously watched the duo in the rear view mirror for some clue.

"You can just pull up to the gates. We'll get out there."

"Lieutenant, how are you going to get in?"

Pete glanced over at Frankie wondering the same.

"Not to worry, Shipmate. We'll get to where we are supposed to be."

With that, Frankie pushed the door open and exited. "Thanks for the ride. Can you hang out for a couple of hours? We're not sure how long this will take."

Petty Officer Wax acknowledged the request with a one finger on the brow salute.

"Frankie, what are we doing here?"

"Pete, I'm really not sure."

"Then why?"

"Hey, I'm just as lost as you but trying to figure it out as we go. I feel this attraction, and I'm just going with it."

They looked around to see if any guards were hanging about in the area. Their SEAL training provided the skills to access the cemetery unnoticed by security.

Pete poked Frankie. "What happens next, Sherlock?"

"I don't know, Watson. Just follow me and, well, I don't know."

Pete had the utmost faith in Frankie. After all, they had been in some pretty brutal battles where mutual trust led to survival, but this night was very different. They weren't in battle, and for all practical purposes, Frankie was presumably dead. Confused but trusting was the best explanation that Pete could muster to justify his going forward.

They made their way up the pathways toward the amphitheater. They had been there a hundred times before paying respects to fallen soldiers of wars gone by. Their youth lent no personal associations with the majority of residents in Arlington, but their incredible bond of "warrior" gave sacred meaning to these grounds.

When Pete and Frankie were measured by others, they were the elite. Inside they carried great humility in their hearts. Their sensitivity towards the sacrifices made and the families left behind by so many others was not lost on them. Even though they were tough-assed fighters of the nth degree, they still cried for the men who had fearlessly charged the beaches of Normandy or dropped from aircraft as floating targets, taking fire without the option to return same.

Frankie would always make a stop and leave a token of gratitude at Audie Murphy's gravesite. He was amazed at the feats this superhuman had accomplished. After all the years that have passed since his death, tens of thousands still come annually to honor this hero. The daily garnishes of roses, notes, coins, and patches serve as a testament to his stature. Military men and women dream about taking out bunkers single-handedly and filling their chests with medals of greatness. Just to be there with his spirit filled their hearts with love for this humble patriot. It's what kids learned while playing army with their friends.

Pete's earliest recollection of Arlington was likened to a distant, foggy dream. He vaguely remembered, as a child, playing among the markers and picnicking with his mom. He didn't give much thought as to why his father hadn't joined them.

Frankie waited while Pete stood there with his 90-mile stare aimed at the white marbled stones.

"Pete, are you with me, pal?"

"Sure."

Frankie pointed over to the crest of the hill.

"There he is."

"Who?"

"Audie."

With a right oblique, he headed in the direction of his hero. Pete followed close behind. As usual, Audie had been recently visited by admirers. There lay a rose atop his stone, and another dozen on the ground. There were patches from Army infantry and small U.S. flags stuck in the dirt. Stacked on top, under the rose, were three coins. Each coin represented platoons that had recently seen action abroad. Frankie reverently bowed, with a wide smile of pride in this man.

"It's awesome, huh?"

Pete couldn't argue that of the most decorated soldier ever.

Frankie validated his point. "Most young men would love to have known Marilyn Monroe. My dream was to meet Audie Murphy."

Pete shook his head. "Frankie, you need therapy."

Pete couldn't wrap his head around this surreal evening. Why were they here? How was Frankie walking and talking like this was an ordinary evening? Pete wasn't getting any answers from his friend. The only relief for Pete was that no matter how tough this evening was, it was better than trying to provide comfort to the families at Andrews. He became somber, drifting off again to a faraway thought.

"Pete."

Pete's mind raced back to the present. "What?"

Frankie waved. "Let's go to the amphitheater."

As they crested the hill, they stopped in their tracks. At that moment, they witnessed the unimaginable.

Pete was stupefied. "Holy crap!"

Frankie seemed at ease with it all. Before them walked hundreds of soldiers, sailors, marines, and airmen dressed in the uniforms of many wars past. Pete's gasp echoed through the valley and caught the attention of the troops. The wonder set in motion a quest to get answers.

Frankie put his hand on Pete's shoulder. "I love this!"

Pete stood silently to assess the sight.

The delegation of warriors milling about the headstones seemed to be relaxed and unaffected by the two intruders watching from above. Pete and Frankie could hear their voices. They were somewhat inaudible and with the air of a chanting-like murmur. The eyes of each of the two spectators grew wider with curiosity as they tried to decipher the garb and medals for a clue of who these servicemen were.

45

"Holy shit, Frankie. That guy has three purple hearts, a Navy Cross and a CMH."

Pete kept tracking the movement of one Marine as he walked about the others greeting and smiling.

"I must say, Pete, that this is pretty damn amazing. I think we have a front row seat to many years of bravery at its finest."

They continued to watch the gathering, not really knowing what would happen next. The sea of servicemen began to form up, steadily moving toward the amphitheater. Pete and Frankie remained in their covert mode to observe, analyze, and calculate what the next move might be. They were trained on assessing before moving forward, but not with what faced them now.

They stood silently. Pete was caught up in the moment and trying to make sense of Frankie's resurrection. Frankie stood silent and proud that he was spectator to a phenomenon unlike any that he had ever dreamed of. The only thing that could top this would be if Audie Murphy were there to greet him. After all, this night was one that was quickly becoming priceless by any measure.

The last of the groups were filing into the amphitheater. The last soldier in line turned, looking directly at the duo. He winked, and then waved them to follow. Pete and Frankie were surprised that anyone even noticed them. They looked at each other, nodded, and followed his direction.

Pete seemed a little on edge. "Do you think they knew we were here all this time?"

"Not sure. I really don't know what to expect when we get in there."

"Hey Frankie, I thought you knew what this night was about."

"Pete, I never said that. I only have this feeling, and it keeps drawing me in this direction."

They walked toward the arena, with both reservation and excitement. This night would not end without their getting answers. The curiosity of what and who was only surpassed by the why of it all. Pete was less at ease now, knowing that Frankie was unsure of the outcome. Still, he kept blindly trudging forward for closure. The anxiety grew in concert with the approaching arena façade. A slight wind created additional shadows of their steps.

The suspense heightened like none they had ever experienced before, including their dark nights of invisible foes in the mountains of Afghanistan. What would be waiting for them at the top of the stairs? They could hear the voices ramping up with each passing footstep. The journey here was filled with shadows of the night, but ahead they could see brightness like day pouring through the marble pillars.

Within a few feet of the top, Pete grabbed his compadre's arm. "Right now my mind is going back to the final scene of Butch Cassidy and the Sundance Kid."

At that moment, they broke the plane and came into full view of the stadium. Standing tall at the top were two young boys in fatigues, guarding the secrets of the night. Frankie and Pete stopped short of the young soldiers and gave them a once over. They could tell that these two innocent warriors were filled with the experience of war. Each wore a uniform of the First World War Era, with many personal and unit awards across his chest.

The younger man on the left was not much over five foot tall, skinny, and maybe 20 years of age. He had bright red hair and an Irish smile that could ingratiate even the cruelest of enemies. His partner, just as young, seemed a little grumpy about our arrival. He was dark haired, with brown eyes that seemed to mimic those of a tough Italian mobster.

Truly, their ages may have been a detriment to them in battle; however, looking at their badges of honor, they were a threat to be reckoned with. Needless to say, Pete and Frankie respected their credentials and paid no attention to their youth. The modern warriors were smart enough to fear the heart of the soldier, not the cover. They each reminded Frankie of his hero Audie, young and fearless, fighting from his heart for his country. They exchanged smiles and handshakes.

In unison the young soldiers welcomed Pete and Frankie. "Glad you boys came."

It seemed strange that these two young whippersnappers would call them boys when they were almost ten years older. When you figure that the two young masters at arms had probably been born around 1925, then they had the right to address Pete and Frankie with a youthful salutation.

Breaking the ice, Frankie was the first to respond. "We really don't know why we are here."

Pete was beckoned back to the present by the cheers of the group. "What?"

Frankie nudged Pete. "Pay attention."

Major Charlie Meyer, a highly decorated Air Force Major and WWII B-25 Bomber pilot, was addressing the group. His words were tough but compassionate. It took only a couple of minutes before Pete and Frankie connected with his message. This war-fighter had a chest filled with medals, the most prestigious around his neck. It was the honored blue ribbon with tiny white stars above a bronze colored star, with an eagle above the word Valor. He was one of the most revered in Arlington.

"Whoever is selected for this mission will need to keeps his wits about him in this theater of battle. It's quite different from what most of us remember. The enemy does not respect life and doesn't have the wholesome values that we used to enjoy when we walked among the living."

Pete chimed, "Yeah."

The group looked at Pete for a moment and then turned back to the speaker.

"I'm talking about why we fought and what brought us here to Arlington."

"I . . ."

Pete gasped. "Holy Moly! Is that . . . ?"

Frankie smiled big. "Yes, I believe it is."

A young airman pointed toward the center of the arena. "He will provide the mission details sir."

Before he could utter the next syllable, the crowd turned toward the parting masses. A figure made his way down to the front, stepping out of the shadows. Pete and Frankie gazed ahead to see a young Navy Lieutenant walk in from a side staircase. At the moment he entered, everyone rose to his or her feet with a resounding, "Attention on Deck!" emanating from the walkway above. Frankie and Pete stopped halfway down to respond to the call to attention. They finally made out the likeness of the Lieutenant as he moved closer.

They stood silent, paralyzed in disbelief, watching the likeness of a much younger President John Kennedy.

The speaker stood straight and smartly saluted. "Good evening, Sir."

Adulation emanated throughout the crowd. This was hard for Frankie and Pete to swallow. It was a thrill that had been enjoyed by men and women every night since November 22, 1963. As a humble man, John Kennedy, or JFK, as many called him, preferred the comfort of his Navy khakis, which represented the office of which he was most proud. He always said that title was earned for life.

"Lieutenant Leonardo, Petty Officer Baker, I'm Jack Kennedy."

They responded. "Yes, Sir!"

Each remained braced at attention in the presence of the most historic figure they would ever hope to meet.

"It's great to have you here, men, and representing the elite sort of Special Forces that I envisioned during my Presidency."

Frankie eloquently submitted, "Good evening, Lieutenant."

Pete stammered, "Mr. President."

He quickly regrouped and followed Frankie's lead, "Excuse me. Good evening, Lieutenant."

JFK smiled. He forgave the newbies, allowing them time to become familiar with his presence.

JFK looked to Frankie. "Lt. Leonardo?"

"Yes, Sir."

"I guess you have Petty Officer Baker in tow for a reason?"

"Yes, Sir."

"And that would be?"

"I'm not real sure, Sir."

"Pete. May I call you Pete?"

"Absolutely, Sir."

"Do you understand why you are here?"

"No."

Jack responded with a big grin. "It's pretty simple. We have our own "occupy movement" going on. The best part is that nobody screws with us. We aren't visible to the regulars who come this way. It provides us with an element of surprise. However, once we are out of the cemetery confines, we have the ability to either be seen or remain unseen."

The duo wasn't sure what to expect next. This was one of those instances that Navy SEAL training had not prepared them for. Pete and Frankie kept exchanging glances to verify that the other was actually there sharing the same experience. Pete wondered if this were all a dream, or whether he had died and gone to heaven to join other fallen veterans. For the most part, they were speechless. They were on this ride, that at times begged them to get off, but more often it kept their curiosity to see what would happen next.

JFK continued. "It's pretty simple, Shipmates. The warriors of today struggle with fighting and serving their country. Many times they can't seem to make sense of it all. We are here to come out from the shadows to instill in them the courage and heart to stay the course. It all became pretty clear when I was on PT-109 and needed the strength to go forward. There seemed to be this force pulling me along, pushing me beyond what I believed myself capable of. That force was the men and women before me. It's what makes up the traditional celebrations and memorials that line the tapestry of our heritage."

Pete raised his hand. "So, you are saying that wherever we are, you are there?"

"Precisely. You may not see us as you do now, but we are always there pushing and shoving for what we believed in. Amazingly, we don't have to push that hard. There are only a few cases when leadership becomes confused and can't articulate the purpose of its being. We help them too, although many times the politicians just don't get it, unless they have walked in our footsteps. I have talked to countless fallen soldiers of wars, both prior to and those who fell after my death. They all confessed spiritual incidents of one sort or another, and they always stopped short of understanding until they became one of us. It's inherent in every warrior to rescue and mend broken things. We are driven by some force that cannot be explained. But damn, it's the most fantastic feeling."

Pete asked, "So, why can I see you now?"

"You have had a couple of troubled times in your life. One, you never understood but will find out before the end of this journey, and two, you have an unfinished life at home with your folks. You will still have time to fix that. We are going to work backward from whence you came with Lt. Leonardo. You have been over the top with grief for, and have not found the right words to say to his widow or son. It's your raw emotion and love for your friend that have brought you here."

"What do you mean, backward?"

"Just that. We will get a group together to go back to Afghanistan to the site of the battle that claimed Frankie's life. The group will be made up of five of the finest."

JFK smiled. "Well, it will be a team with intense determination. You get to pick the crew, and as incentive, we reward those you choose by letting them go home to finish their lives. You know, curiosity is a mighty powerful tool. Some are afraid to go home, and then there are others who run home at the speed of light. Either way, you will make some fallen friends mighty appreciative."

JFK spoke to bystanders. "Most of the guys and gals wonder whether the price they paid was really worth it. Did they make a difference? Are their families okay? Unfortunately, many assume that they were forgotten by the ones they left behind. I can assure you that I don't believe that's the case."

He turned back toward Pete. "The five you choose will hopefully find comfort and ease their restless hearts."

Pete shrugged his shoulders. "What's next?"

JFK replied. "That would be to finish the mission that left Lt. Leonardo lifeless."

Pete and Frankie thought about JFK's words. If the two of them had been able to pass into this spiritual world, then many other questions would follow. They began asking themselves those questions that preceded every mission. Did they make a difference in someone's life? Was their contribution to their country worth the price of losing it all? For Frankie, was it fair to leave a widow and a son to the vestiges of today's world without his continued love and support?

Pete wasn't out of the pool of regret. Although hadn't bailed on a widow or child, his shame was just as heavy. He had left his parents begging at their door for his understanding, and then never answered the follow-on letters asking for forgiveness. His continued evasion was not how he felt, but would he have a chance to make it right? He just needed one more day to see them.

OLD RECRUITS,
NEW RECRUITS

JFK pointed to the waves of spirited warriors. "Okay Pete, take your pick."

He explained to Pete and Frankie. "We get fallen veterans from other parts of the world. Those are the comrades who never made it back to American soil. It's an opportunity for them to cross their mamas' doorsteps, or just to see our great land again. They have traveled from the depths of the *U.S.S. Arizona* and from Normandy, just to name a couple. We try to convince them that they played a truly important part in the history of this fine nation. After all, what good is the gift of death if it doesn't change the outcome of history?"

Jack pointed in the direction of the Capitol. "Some just don't get the strength and honor code. I haven't seen them sponsor the first 'in your face' story of a soldier not coming home, or the real pain of the family who has to go on without them. Their reason to bring the troops home is for v o t e s. It's normally after great, unnecessary loss that they finally make a decision. Perhaps if they or their sons and daughters were in combat, it would have a greater and more meaningful priority."

The face of every soldier seemed to be sedulously echoing his pain. Pete looked to the masses, glancing over his shoulder toward Jack. "What's next?"

"Pick your team."

"Sir, I don't feel qualified, and I don't think that I can be fair."

"Why not?"

Pete shrugged. "Too young?"

JFK challenged his comment. "Pete, the youngest Medal of Honor recipient was Willie Johnston. He earned his award at age 11 in 1862. Over there is Jack Lucas. At age 17, this Marine shielded fellow squad members from grenades at Iwo Jima. You're 26 with a lot more advanced military education, so choosing winners from a group of heroes isn't all that difficult. Your choices will give five souls their chances to check on family and ease their souls about home."

Frankie put his arm around Pete, and with a supportive cheer said, "C'mon Shipmate, I'll help you."

"Thanks Frankie."

They began looking around at the faces of the men and women. In each face they saw certain emptiness. The hollow look in their faces was reminiscent of those that you see in lost loves. Each had his or her own story, but each one of them at some time had had a family.

Pete reflected on his own life and the family he had left behind on purpose. He had been so filled with anger for his family that there hadn't been room to be lonely. His family had become the SEAL Team. He would soon find out more about life than he had ever bargained for.

"Well, where do we begin, Pete?"

"I don't know. I'm way under qualified for this mission. It's easier to plan normal mission ops, but this is much more daunting. We're messing with real people's lives. Well, maybe not real."

"Remember, this is the same mission, second attempt, so we have the known. We can't lollygag for too long because Sara and Austin are waiting on the flight line back at Andrews. If we don't hurry, they will be chasing an empty coffin through D.C. She'd probably get stuck in the pissed off/ hurt position."

Pete knew that his duty was to be with Frankie's family at the aircraft's arrival. This part of the equation was way beyond where Pete and Frankie were dealing from. They were stuck in the present and being given orders by a dead President.

Jack looked sternly at Pete. "You need to choose."

About 50 unsettled souls stepped closer in an attempt to be considered for the right to return to their pre-war lives.

Pete turned back to Jack. "I just can't do it, Sir."

"It wasn't a request, Pete."

Frankie chuckled. "Yup, this is your party, Pete."

"The challenge is daunting, Sir. They should all get to go home."

Frankie offered his little pearl of wisdom. "Don't think of it as passing up thousands, look at the few who get the miracle."

"Frankie, you're definitely not in the position to offer help. You left your two miracles at home."

"You're wasting time, Pete. Just follow your heart."

JFK was getting tired of their exchange. "Frankie's right. You will find every warrior here would give his spot for another. That's how we're made. It's not so easily understood by others. There's a gene we carry inherent to tending to, and risking all for another in uniform. It's what we do. It's what you do."

Pete gazed around to see the longing in their eyes. The soldiers waited. Some were eager to do the mission and return home. Others would refuse the opportunity to go home; afraid to find that someone has taken their places, or that they wouldn't even be remembered. To have never existed in another's life that they knew as their own was their greatest fear. In just about every instance, the idea would relegate them to a wistful state of being.

They continually dreamed of self-actualizing. Silently, they saw their worlds fall apart because they hadn't been there. Or, their loyal spouses refused to date again because there could never be a better man or woman than them. Just like buying a lotto ticket. You know you won't win, but the allure and perfect day setting make you smile. Hope was a small gift to those who gave their lives for their country. To always be remembered in someone's heart as "the" only ticket to eternal happiness was their dream.

The thoughts of their choices haunted most. Why would they give the gift of life for a sometimes thankless nation? That seemed a poor choice, rather than attending your child's graduation or giving your little girl away as a bride-to-be. Possibly, the living world was dead, and the dead were witnessing life with such an unrequited love for everyone, and for their being. What a great mantra to be giving without condition. Perhaps they learned after their chances had escaped them.

Pete's potential recruits were glowing with anticipation to see a spouse, a girlfriend, and maybe the smile of a child. They had waited for decades and beyond for the chance to go home. The barely audible moan of prayers was killing Pete. This was an incredible responsibility that no one should ever bear alone.

Pete grabbed Frankie and walked away from the group. He turned his face away from the men with his hands on Frankie's shoulders.

"Help me, Frankie."

"Take it easy, Pete."

"I don't know what to say or do. I'm a damn mess. I couldn't come up with something simple to say to Sara and Austin about you. I failed even that. Now I'm responsible for five lives, and that outcome!"

Pete broke away from Frankie and began to walk in a circle.

Frankie attempted to console Pete.

"You haven't failed. Just take one at a time. I'm sure it will come to you. They are all deserving, so it's easy to pick a winner. Follow your heart. We're waiting on you. Honestly, I'm looking forward to shooting that asshole that clipped me. Then I'm going to see Sara one last time."

Pete wiped his tears and returned to the task.

Frankie whispered. "I got your back, Brother."

Pete walked gingerly through the crowd. Most cut their eyes away from him to avoid contact. They believed that they would be chosen by fate and not by campaigning. There were some who portrayed "puppy dog eyes" without trying. After all, many had walked Arlington for decades dreaming about this once-in-a-lifetime occasion.

Pete scanned the many wannabee home-goers as he walked, finding it near impossible to pick one out of so many deserving souls. He was trying to transform his nerves to numbness to make this task less daunting.

What seemed forever to him was, in reality, only a few minutes. As he saw a few old Sailors, he recalled a visit to Pearl Harbor two years earlier. He had openly wept as he watched the oil seep to the top of the stack of the submerged *U.S.S. Arizona*. Many old-timers believe that the reddish oil is really the blood from the sailors in the ship below, and serves as a reminder that they are still there, wanting to get out. Pete had those same images years earlier of them walking the decks below.

He was fortunate to have watched the rare event of a Pearl Harbor Marine Veteran, who had been stationed aboard the *USS Arizona*, being interred by Navy divers inside the ship in his final resting place. This was an honor restricted to those veterans of that day and that ship.

Pete often thought about the 1,102 *Arizona* residents below, and that they never saw the light of day again. If only he could have raised the ship, the men, and sent them home again. Well, this was his moment to grant the wish to at least one. Without hesitation, he commanded everyone's attention.

"Gents, are there any *U.S.S. Arizona* shipmates out there?"

He was all eyes and ears, hopeful that he would hear "yes." He couldn't muster one response from the hundreds there. JFK smirked, and then winked at Frankie. He knew that the prayer would be answered. Sure enough, a salty Chief Petty Officer swaggered down the walkway. His cover was tilted to one side, and he rolled a stogie around his mouth in the fashion of Edward G. Robinson. Pete leaned forward in anticipation, nodding his head, waiting for the Chief to say something, anything.

"Chief?"

The Chief smiled. "Petty Officer Baker? I'm Chief Boatswains Mate, Charlie Koberlein."

"You're from the *U.S.S. Arizona*?"

"In the flesh. Well, not really in the flesh, but in spirit."

Pete smiled huge. He was honored to meet someone whom he held in such regard; someone who saw it all, and never got to go home. This was Pete's time to make it happen, and it was this instance that would morph this nervous, unsure young man into a force that would soon catch the attention of the crowd.

"Chief Koberlein, what an honor, Sir."

"You call me sir again, and I'll kick your ass."

"Sorry, Chief. You know, I've always dreamed of getting you poor bastards out of that hull. Did you have a girlfriend, a wife, and children?"

"No, not any of those."

Pete cocked his head.

"So, what did you leave behind?"

"I left a great family. A mom, dad, and sister, who loved me very much. Between listening to the bitching and whining below decks, I would sit alone and think about the folks. I couldn't imagine the pain that they lived with after the bombing. I bet that it took years for them to figure out if I had survived the attack."

"Well, Chief, you can go back after the mission to find out, and to soothe their pain."

"Can you count?"

Pete asked, "Yes, why?"

"2013 minus 1941 equals 72. Now, add 72 to 55. That's 127. If you do the math, I don't think that they are still with us."

"Sorry."

"You might be better picking someone whose family is still around."

"Maybe your sister is still alive."

"Helen? Maybe."

"She could tell you how life went on after your death. I bet Helen could answer the questions you've had for all these years."

"I'm not sure that I would want to know."

Charlie had never had the pleasure of a lady in his life, and never enjoyed the pitter-patter of rug rats around his home. He had always focused on his mother and father in a down-home environment. His beliefs had always been centered on God, country, strength, and honor of service to country.

His naval service emulated the pattern set by the hard core Navy Boatswains Mates who believed that "if it didn't come in a sea bag, then you didn't need it." He had hidden his deep devotion to his immediate family and exuded the tough exterior while haze gray and underway. Within his façade, though, beat a heart of tenderness, sensitivity, and love for home. He could never hide his true feelings from his family, no matter how hard he tried. He knew that his rough exterior never made muster with his folks, and conceded that their pain of losing him would be without equal.

For all the years that Charlie had spent in the bowels of the *Arizona*, anchored below Pearl Harbor, he had hoped that his family would heal quickly and move on to find a better tomorrow. His reality was that he couldn't convince himself of that miracle, and that sorrow would fill their lives till the day they died. Helen, if she were still alive, would be the only person who could attest to their getting through the pain, and consequently ease the pain in his heart. After all, he had felt the blast for a moment and then lay at peace below. They were the ones who would have had to endure what probably seemed to them an eternity.

Pete challenged Charlie. "Why not?"

Charlie had prayed many times that Helen would have gotten married and possibly named a son after him. That would be a new center for his parents' universe, which would have eased their torment. To him it was just another hope that he kept alive below decks on that steel tomb. Going back home, seeing Helen would be the only way that he could ever find the answers. Charlie became more convinced to take Pete's offer.

"Pete, I think you are on to something. The only peace for me would be to find the truth, and the only way to do that is to talk to Helen."

Pete was relieved. He had found his first recruit, and this recruit was tough as nails. He couldn't believe that a little common sense and humble dialogue had persuaded the crusty "Old Salt" to come his way.

Frankie glanced over at Pete, rolled his eyes, and smiled. Pete returned his approval with the same and began to show greater self-confidence. He quickly realized that his choices would become more human-based rather than based on the mission, but the ultimate selection would be a warrior with incredible heart.

Pete continued toward the front of the group, noticing an Army Corporal wearing the Medal of Honor. The Corporal maintained his attention toward the ground. Pete stopped head on, and tapped him on the shoulder. He noted that the Corporal was about the same age as he.

"Corporal, it looks like you've been to hell and back."

The Corporal looked up with a humbleness that suggested his spirit had been beaten down.

"Where did you fight, Corporal?"

"Omaha Beach."

Pete tried to analyze his mannerisms to establish a connection. His dog tags were hanging out just enough to reveal his name.

"Tony Burr?"

"Yes."

"Where are you from?"

"Great Falls, Montana."

"Did you have a girl there?"

Tony's eyes lit up, and he smiled. That question piqued his interest. "Yup."

Pete realized that pulling information out of this one might be a much greater challenge than it had been with Charlie. He was afraid that the next question might be as dangerous as pulling a tiger's tail.

"So, Tony, do you think that the little lady is waiting back there in Great Falls?"

Tony's smile departed his face and sadness became him. Pete began to backstep his words. He was filled with remorse over what he had asked the Corporal and was quick to reassure Tony that she was there, waiting.

"Tony, I am sure that she's perched on the porch waiting for her soldier to return. What is her name?"

He looked up at Pete with reservation that perhaps she hadn't waited. Tony remembered his final words to her. "Don't wait for me." Then he recalled her promise that she would be right there, forever. Tony was back and forth in his heart and in his mind, whether she remained or moved forward with another.

"Her name is Ruth."

Pete smiled as he tried to engage Tony's positive side. He knew that hope would be the greatest incentive to encourage the recruits to go home. Just as he had with Charlie, Pete wanted the Corporal's future to appear believable. However, the mere thought of these spirits being replaced by another in their former lives brought panic to their souls.

Many passing years of self-reflection had taught the veterans a great deal about themselves. They had had an abundance of time and countless seasons of solitude after death to recall events in their lives. They wondered how they could have done life differently. Every story was unique, and at times, incredibly heartbreaking. They speculated whether they had been forgiven for acts that at the time seemed inconsequential to them. Above all, they pleaded with their God to have the opportunity to get another chance to do it differently.

Pete's thoughts rushed him like the oncoming troops at Normandy, crowding him with a million "what-if's." It was apparent that he would do much better selling these enlightened spirits with a second chance at redemption. It would be their break to put down the baggage they had carried for so many years.

"Tony, do you have any regrets?"

"No."

"Okay, let's say that Ruth is there waiting. What would you say to her after all these years?"

"Not much of anything."

"Wasn't there something that you should have done differently?"

"No."

Pete wasn't getting anywhere in this conversation, so he gave Tony a thumbs up and said, "So, we're good to go?"

"I guess."

Pete placed his hand on Tony's shoulder.

"I'll bet she's waiting."

Tony smiled.

Pete moved on, and he noticed an Air Force Major who had been fidgeting the entire time that he had been talking with Tony. The Major had kept eye contact with Pete during his entire exchange with Tony, and he seemed very anxious. Pete stepped directly to him and glanced at his name tag.

"Major Rick Wood, I'm Petty Officer Pete Baker."

"I know. I've been listening to you trying to convince Tony to go home after our mission."

"Yes, and?"

"Well, you could have saved your breath with him. He's all about hooking up with Ruthie. We've had to hear Romeo go on and on and on about his love life. Everyone was hoping that he would go just to leave us with some peace at night."

Ricky smiled, looked at Tony, and gave him a "thumbs up."

"You won't have to sell me. I'm a ready teddy. I've dreamed of this day ever since the last bombing run over Vietnam. I want to go home. I have so much to say to my family."

"Like what?"

"Like what an unworthy father and husband I was."

"In what way?"

"I was so caught up in the war that I pushed my family aside. I moved out of the house emotionally one year before I went back to Vietnam. For some unknown reason, I guess my gut kept telling me that I wasn't coming back, so it was my way to cut ties to ease their pain of the loss."

"I'm sure that they understood your predicament and have forgiven you."

"How could they? My children were five and six."

All the nightmares that he had had since that time began flooding Ricky's head, and he just wanted them to go away.

"I'm sure your wife explained to the children why you were so removed."

"That's the part that I feel so badly about."

Rick's eyes welled up, and he sighed. He reeked of remorse for deeds in his past. You could see his pain through his actions. He held his head, and then began combing his hands through his hair, as if he wanted to pull it out.

"I've committed the most heinous crime in life. I cast my family out of my life to ease my selfish suffering. I abandoned them during the most crucial time in their lives. I'm ashamed to even think about it, much less talk about it."

Pete stopped Rick's rant, standing over him with a hand of calm on his shoulder.

"I think we all carry guilt about things we did or didn't do, especially those whose lives get cut short. They never get the chance to correct their course, and the families grow to forgive and forget."

"Not as deeply as I hurt them."

"Major, I split with my folks on some pretty bad terms. They begged me to go to college, and I wanted to enlist. I could read it in my mama's eyes as I walked away. My parents had always been great to me; however, in a fit of independence, I chose to walk."

"You're still sucking air Pete, and able to fix it."

"I'm not so sure about that. I'm still pretty pissed that they didn't respect my ideals."

"Petty fits your rank, and your rationale."

Pete looked down and away from the Major. He knew that Ricky Wood was spot on in his assessment, but Pete's pig-headedness would always win over his intellect, even when it came to doing the right thing.

"Okay, Major. We can do the mission and then find out your truth."

"Sounds good to me. My family has had over forty years to move on. I'll be lucky if they remember that I ever existed."

"They'll remember, and you can thank them for the time they spent with you."

"Yes, and I will certainly take the chance to do what I should have done forty three years ago, and that was to kiss them goodbye."

Pete smiled and gripped Ricky's hand.

"So, we're good?"

Ricky stood up and stared at Pete intently to communicate that he was accepting the challenge. He smiled, gripping Pete's hand like a vise.

"Yep, we're good."

Pete sighed. "Okay."

They began to feel the special bond of brotherhood and understanding that was inherent in most warriors of similar service.

Pete cut his eyes in Frankie's direction, looking for some sign of approval.

Frankie looked back and mouthed, "Kudos."

Pete was distracted by all the chatter in the crowd. He watched JFK approach Ricky as if to reinforce Pete's discussion with him.

Pete took a couple of minutes to stand alone. His disrespectful demeanor toward his parents had begun to surface while he was talking with Ricky. He recalled that he never hugged his parents or said goodbye to them on the day of his hostile departure. He was hiding secrets on the outside, but inside, he began falling apart. He knew that he couldn't display weakness in front of all these warriors.

Frankie's interest in his friend's quest to find recruits was gaining momentum and spirit.

"C'mon, Pete. We don't have all day."

Pete composed himself before searching for the next selectee. He was in deep thought and shuffled his feet up the walkway. By this time, the adrenaline rush was gone, and he felt the sleep agents calling his name. He stopped and looked around the cemetery. His intention was to move out of hearing distance of those already chosen in order to evade any ridicule.

Pete hated to be mocked, and that seemed to be a sport of the Arlington residents since there wasn't much else to do. Most teasing was based on service rivalry, but at times they could be pretty hurtful when talking about others' personal lives. Warfighters were hard men and women who endured great pain at home and on the field. There wasn't a lot of compassion as a group, but individually the benevolence was great.

Pete targeted nearby laughter in hopes that it would change the present state of solemnness that seemed to be crowding his spirit. He was overdue for some merriment after the past weeks of personal pain. Straight ahead sat a Marine Sergeant laughing and poking fun at the others. He was determined to make the best of what he referred to as his dead time. He was full of himself and entertaining others with his witty humor.

Sergeant Allan Milk had lost his life in Iraq. He was shorter than most and had a strong resemblance to the Polish Prince, better known as Bobby Vinton. Allan whisked his own personal pain away by terrorizing others with witty barbs about their woes. After each combative encounter, he would reach out and pull the victim in for a hug, with a hope to maintain his loyalty to his show. He kept busy living others' lives because he had lost hope that he could ever find his own.

Pete watched as Allan smacked down his latest victim. "What were you thinking?"

Laughter from the crowd followed with the casualty chuckling at himself for his stupid decisions. Pete approached the Sergeant with an ear-to-ear grin. He couldn't remember when he had smiled last. He knew that he was in a better place because he could smile. He assumed that the statistics for frowns at all military cemeteries could never be surpassed if you considered the number of people times the number of heartbreaks times the number of decades passed. He felt it refreshing to feel his cheek muscles work. Pete was hopeful that Sergeant Milk would be an easy mark for the mission.

Sergeant Milk surveyed the group's attention and found it to be in the direction of this approaching living Navy man. He stood up and saluted Pete.

"Navy Squid, arriving."

Allan was great at trying to get the psychological jump on his prey. He was wondering why everyone was looking so intently at this sailor. He had been so obsessed with his own performance, that he was unaware of the recruitment that was taking place.

"Come for some words of wisdom, Sailor? You boys are out of your element. Did you run out of troops to carry across the pond?"

Pete reached out his hand.

"I'm Pete Murphy. Glad to make your acquaintance, Sergeant."

Pete cocked his head in anticipation that the Sergeant would respond in kind. He waited for what seemed to be a couple of minutes. Sergeant Milk stared intently above Pete's left pocket. He realized that this target deserved a little more respect with the trident that he wore. But in his style of staying in his game, he looked up and readied himself for a battle of wits.

"Sergeant Milk?"

"You can call me Allan. We are in the same service, just different departments. I'm in the Men's Department."

Allan smiled and looked around the crowd for approval of his first round with the Petty Officer. Allan knew that he was bantering with a pretty fierce fighter; the best of the best. Pete smiled and retreated three steps. He had erred in thinking that this would be easy. He was beginning to realize that it was easier to convince a battered man to hope than bring a hopeful man back to reality.

"Allan, we need your spirit to help carry a few good men into battle. After which, you will be rewarded by being able to return to the life that you left unexpectedly."

"Oh really? And how do I fit in after more than ten years have passed?"

Allan's entire demeanor changed from pleasure to pain.

"Don't you know that I have thought about this for all these years?"

"Yes."

"What could I possibly bring to my past life that has since been filled with other people, other pleasures? This is a joke, right? I'm not even this cruel to others, so why are you doing this to me?"

"Allan, I don't know what brought me to you, but there has to be something you are supposed to do, or someone that you are supposed to help."

"Do pray tell."

Pete was caught off guard by Allan's sudden change in character. Allan's face reddened and his composure escaped him. Pete stopped and contemplated for a few moments, hoping that the words would magically roll off his tongue.

"Allan."

Pete then stood silently waiting for Allan's next move. It was a courteous gesture on Pete's part to let Allan gather his thoughts to move the conversation forward. The silence was deafening. Pete wasn't about to walk off looking for another recruit for the mission. He was like a dog with a bone. It was becoming his personal challenge to convince the Sergeant to accept the mission, come hell, or high water. Frankie stood away to the side, grinning. He knew how Pete was wired. On many occasions Frankie had told Pete that he'd rather be stupid than be wrong.

Pete took a moment longer to collect his thoughts and then proceeded. "Okay."

Pete really didn't have a plan of what he would say next, but as he had hoped, Allan opened the door for him to walk through.

"What?" Allan asked

Pete was ready. "Did you leave any unfinished business at home?"

This dialogue was foreign to Allan. He was always joking and certainly not used to answering to a squid in front of the crowd that he normally mocked into submission. Again, he stood silently, wanting to share but afraid of showing a sensitive side.

Allan pointed. "Can we talk over there?"

Pete motioned for Allan to lead the way. Allan lowered his head in defeat, making his way over to a stone bench under a tree. The crowd was astute enough not to make light of this conversation. Frankie stayed behind to ease their communication. He was impressed that Pete was coming into his own and gaining the confidence to rally with the best. He was watching a young man mature right in front of his eyes, and he was pleased that Pete's hard line on issues was softening with others. Maybe it was Pete's respect for these fallen and the sacrifices that they had made, or maybe it was that he realized that he was running out of chances in his own life.

Allan and Pete stood toe to toe as they began their discussion.

Allan confessed to Pete. "I have to distract their attention from the lives that they left. If I don't, they will bring the mood down to rock bottom, further perpetuating their depression, leaving them in total despair. I can't stand the magnitude of sadness that emanates throughout the hills of this place. Every person here was shorted, cheated from living his or her dream. Instead, they exist in this constant nightmare of what could have been."

"I understand."

"I don't think you do."

Pete then abstained. He shook his head north and south, and listened intently.

Allan continued. "There are so many stories here that I could write to life. Get it? Write to life? My story pales in comparison to most of these. Many left behind several children. So, if you take the sorrow of the wife and multiply it times the numbers of kids, now that becomes unbearable. When these guys figure that out, they can't die from heartbreak, because they're already dead. They are doomed to have restless hearts forever."

Pete nodded his head yes.

"Allan, I am offering you a chance to bring closure to your life."

"Why me, Pete? I only had a wife. I didn't have kids, and I spent most of the last ten years before my death away from my immediate family. So, the pain of separation wasn't as great for them."

"There is a reason that I came to you, Allan. I can't explain it. I don't know why. Perhaps it's your chance to go home and finish your life so that you can come back here to share happiness and hope with the others. You do have the flare for entertaining and communicating. Wouldn't it be grand to strip away the regret from those here? I believe that's the wound that can never be healed completely, or at best a battle scar that remains for eternity."

"I don't know how I could do all of that."

"You have a gift to captivate and communicate. You could be the greatest hero to ever walk these hills. To save so many would bring a joy that you never believed possible."

They sat silent in thought for a few minutes trying to digest the entire dialogue. Pete still wondered about Allan and what made him tick. Allan's mind was going a hundred miles an hour trying to figure out how he could help the others. At the same time, he was contemplating what it would be like to see Donna. How had she been and what had her life been like over the last ten years? More importantly, did she miss him? So many powerful thoughts passed through his mind at once, complicating what his next words would be.

Pete didn't know what Allan would be going back to. He was ready to argue the points that Allan's return home would ultimately change the world of Arlington Cemetery. Perhaps Allan would find that all was okay at home and give that glimmer of hope to others. They were both emotionally exhausted and out of time to sit much longer.

"Well?"

"I would love to see her."

"Who?"

"Donna."

"How long did you know her before you went to Iraq?"

"We knew each other since kindergarten. We started passing notes in elementary school. We held hands when the teachers weren't watching and stole kisses under the stairwell at class change in junior high. I gave her my class ring in our senior year just to keep others away. She was gorgeous. She was the Prom Queen, and I was the King. We'd work together on my folks' farm in Cochecton. We fished and canoed the Delaware River, and hiked the Catskill Mountains. Pretty much, we did everything together, all the time."

"What made you leave?"

"Nine-Eleven. I loved my country so much and couldn't bear those bastards encroaching on my dream. We were only 70 miles from New York City, and that was too close for me and too close to my sweetie's safety zone."

"Well, that was honorable."

Pete could see that he had struck another nerve.

"It was nuts. I had it all, a wife and a great life. I gave all of it up for honor."

"It was the noble thing to do."

"Bullshit. Look at me now. Look at those guys."

Allan's ire rose as he saw his friends sitting around with nowhere to go and no loved ones to be with. Pete had no rebuttal. His mind was tracking a hundred miles a minute.

"If it weren't for you and them we wouldn't be a free nation. Perhaps the terrorists would be rampant on the streets of New York City. You can't minimize your contribution to our freedom. It's why I'm here. It's why I am following the lead of others before me."

"Again, bull!"

"Allan, we will never know whether we are doing the right thing unless you and the others go home to find the truth. It's never been done, and this is our chance to find out. What you all left behind was people who loved you and believed in you. I'm betting that they believed in your choices and still support that in their hearts. I believe that you haven't been forgotten and will never be forgotten. In fact, let's look up your name on my phone."

"Look up what?"

"Oh, this is a smart phone. I can look up your information on the internet."

"No kidding."

Pete typed in Allan Milk.

"What town in New York?"

"Cochecton."

"Okay, here it is. The VFW Allan Milk Memorial Post #7276."

"For real?"

A smile filled Allan's face as he grabbed the phone from Pete.

"This is cool. Can you look up Donna?"

"We really need to move on with the mission. We can look later while we are traveling."

The curiosity was overwhelming now for Allan. He had his name on a VFW Post. What else was in store when he got back home? His anger quickly turned to eager. So, Pete had his last recruit. He watched Allan's step pick up and smiled at his change of heart.

ORDERS

Pete and Allan walked back toward Frankie. Pete signaled with a wink and a nod that he had garnered the fourth recruit. They walked in the direction of the old Arlington Amphitheater. JFK, Chief Koberlein, Corporal Burr, and Major Wood stood in the path awaiting their return. As Pete got closer, he rendered a salute to JFK, while making eye contact with the others. The others returned the salute and smiled.

The excitement was building as they continued the walk up the hill. Everyone was silent during the trip. Pete was still reeling from the reality of what had happened in the last few hours. He walked alongside JFK and couldn't help staring at the iconic treasure. JFK caught him, and stopped.

"Are you okay?"

"Yes, Sir. I don't really know what to think of it all."

"Maybe you should focus on the next event."

"What is that, Sir?"

"Putting the mission together. This time you need to succeed."

"I think we succeeded."

Before the last syllable passed through his lips, he realized that it hadn't been successful at all. It had killed his best friend. Pete looked back at Frankie, then at JFK. It was time for him to prepare for the next step.

They arrived at the old amphitheater. JFK promptly sat down and motioned to Frankie, Charlie, Ricky, Allan, and Tony to sit alongside. He motioned Pete to stand in front and to talk through the points of the mission. JFK hesitated, to wait for Audie Murphy's presence. Regardless of Presidential authority, there was still awe and reverence for the man who was unquestionably a hero's hero. Audie walked up and sat next to

Frankie. Pete stood there with a ninety-mile stare. Audie was the first to break the silence.

"So, Pete, what's it going to be?"

The sound of Audie's voice made Pete shake. He'd been ripped by the best at SEAL training, and in the line of fire on some pretty nasty missions, but he'd never been addressed by someone of this standing.

"Sir?"

"Aren't you taking these men back over to settle a score?"

"Yes, Sir."

"So what's it going to be? Strategy? Firepower . . . ? You know, a plan?"

"Oh."

Pete stood like a new recruit who had never been introduced into battle. From Audie's question, it sounded like the talking was over, and now it was time to roll into action. Audie looked at Pete, then the group, then back at Pete, and smiled.

"I'm playing with you, Pete. Okay, you were already briefed on the mission a month ago. Our spooks at the CIA are saying that the game is still the same as when you guys hit the first time. When I say spooks, I'm talking about our ghostly Intel boys who pour though files at night while others sleep. The only difference on this mission is that you will be supported by a skeleton crew."

The group laughed at the pun.

Audie continued. "Lighten up, Pete. I learned a long time ago to enjoy the ride because you never know when it might be your last."

Audie pointed directly at him, and Pete's eyes flew open wide, thinking that maybe there was an underlying message there.

"You will have everyone here with you on this mission, with the exception of JFK and me. We wouldn't want to steal your thunder. You will have limited troops to provide cover and to get you into position in Afghanistan. The mission remains the same, but the faces have changed."

"How do we get there?"

"The same way that you got here. The plane is still at Andrews. You leave early tomorrow morning."

JFK stood up after Audie had finished and addressed the group.

"Gents, I want to thank you for doing this for Pete, and I want to remind you to keep your wits about you. Don't think about home until you have finished the assignment. Losing focus can cost you your life, and then that would be one less family to get their overdue reunion."

Pete could feel the energy of the group and understood that not only would the success of this mission be a victory for the country, but it would also be a long overdue miracle for the families who had waited so long.

Audie smiled. "Pete, Frankie, I think that you'll especially love working with those crazy-assed Vietnam Vets."

Rick jumped up. "Hear, Hear."

Audie continued. "They will be taking you from the base in Afghanistan to a close proximity of where you'll launch the mission. JFK and I get emotional when we watch the "Rolling Thunder" carrying the torch for their fallen brothers who were ridiculed and forgotten by the very nation that they died for."

JFK echoed Audie's words by way of his famous tooth-filled smile.

Frankie looked to Pete. "Hey, Shipmate. We need to get moving to make the morning flight. Do you think the duty driver is still around?"

"Who knows? We have five of us to get up to Andrews. I guess we'll have to squeeze in."

"Whatever it takes. This mission is all or nothing. I feel the burden of the responsibility of making all this happen, but more so, I feel that if it doesn't happen, I am letting all of these guys down that I just recruited, not to mention their families."

"Yeah, not to mention JFK, and your hero, Audie."

"Thanks . . . no pressure added, right?"

JFK and Audie approached Pete and Frankie.

"We're going to get on down the hill. JFK has some midnight manipulating bedside at 1600 Pennsylvania. The present tenant needs some work, and I've got a meeting at the Pentagon to make adjustments to accommodate the mission. You're on your own now, and with our blessing."

JFK reached out to the boys. "Frankie, Pete, Allan, Tony, Charlie, Rick. God Bless each one of you. I want to hear the stories about home when you get back someday. Frankie, I'll see you back right after the mission. Pete, your time is still up in the air, so use it wisely."

The group exchanged good wishes for success and went their ways.

Frankie never gave it a thought that he wasn't going to be rewarded by going to see Sara and Austin. He realized that he was in between, and that he hadn't even been buried yet. He shook off his disappointment by glad-handing the others that their homecoming opportunity was imminent. He was saddened to his core that he wouldn't hold Sara or play in the sand with Austin. Not only that, but he had to go through the whole flag-covered casket arrival and burial process.

He detested the fact that he would be the audience to his family's pain. Right now, he just wanted to be dead and let them suffer through the whole ordeal without his knowing. Tony was paying particular attention to Frankie and knew, without question, what he was thinking. He was also one to never impart wisdom on others, but he couldn't hold back this time.

"You're a selfish bastard, Frankie."

"What?"

"I know what you're thinking, and all I can say is . . . Really?"

"I . . ."

"So, you want to abandon them twice? The first was in the cards, but this time you can stand next to them, and in spirit, hold their hands through this excruciating ordeal. They didn't ask for this."

Frankie stopped dead in his tracks, turned, and headed over to a marker at the base of a lone tree. The others slowed, giving time for him to collect his thoughts. He sat at the base of the tree in the shadow of a marker. The moon reflected on the stone like a spotlight to Frankie's attention.

"Infant, June 16, 1961, Son of SSgt R J McCann, USAF."

You could best describe his mind as mush at this particular moment. He had just lost his life, his wife and son, his family, and his future, and now he was living a nightmare of things he couldn't comprehend. It was the "Infant" inscription that grabbed him by the throat. He began rambling in a low voice that could only be shared by the gravestone beside him.

"An infant without an identity. He had a father. What about that family? Where are they? Austin has a name, and now doesn't have a father. He has a mother who doesn't have a husband. Is this the first part where I am gone and now separated for eternity from my family? Will Sara end up on a stone with someone else, while I remain alone under a tree? Will

Austin not be with her, or me? What have I done? Will I ever see them? I've given my life and am rewarded with being alone?"

Frankie wept privately while trying to make sense of it all.

"Will my family move on? Do I want them to?"

He knew in his heart that there was not a choice about the future for him. He understood that the only choices would be made by Sara until Austin would make his own, unless he ended up on a marker like this little fella. Those were pretty powerful sad thoughts for Frankie.

Frankie wondered if they had made the decision for him to go in the Navy together, or if it had been all his doing. Was Sara angry with him, or accepting of the way that things turned out? She would have other opportunities to move on and be happy. Frankie wouldn't. This was the end for him. Once again he heard Tony's words echo. Maybe he was a selfish bastard, and now this was his punishment.

He peeked around the tree to see that the others were waiting. The time spent in his pity party was affecting the others' opportunity of going home. But that was a reward that he wouldn't enjoy. So, why should he care? He hid the evidence of weakness on his sleeve, took a couple deep breaths, and headed toward the impatient troops.

Tony was the first to break the ice. "Sorry, Lieutenant."

Frankie quickly rallied. "It's all good."

Pete asked. "Is it?"

"Yep."

They picked up the pace, migrating to the entrance of Arlington. Pete and Frankie marveled at the beauty of the night, with the moon shining on the manicured pathways that were filled with diverse, enduring personalities from the past. They could only imagine the stories shared each evening, and how so many had been affected by the happenstance of life. The intense passion for family and country that these warriors expressed made the air so dense with powerful emotion that it was difficult to walk through. It was hard to walk past every gathering and not stop to hear each storyteller.

During the walk, Charlie shared his weakness for seeking out the ladies who inhabited the cemetery. He had never had time for a wife, having joined the Navy at an early age. He said that we would sit mesmerized by the stories of these women, who he had always thought were the delicate creatures of life, but had since learned that they, too, were strong and courageous. He enjoyed the softer articulation of war stories and a woman's perspective of loves lost and lives cut short. Pete and Frankie were learning at rocket speed that life wasn't all about them, and that women weren't just for loving. The ladies could certainly hold their own and then some.

The glow of the entrance lights got brighter with each step.

"Frankie, there's the van."

"Hell yeah! Where's the duty driver?"

The duty driver had stretched out across the seat and lay sound asleep.

Charlie yelled through the open window. "Off your ass and on your feet, Sailor!"

The Petty Officer, in one quick motion rose up, opened the door, and fell out in front of them.

Half asleep, the duty driver barked, "Good to go!"

Ricky jabbed at him. "Sleeping on watch, Boy?"

"No, Sir."

Tony jumped in. "Looks like it to me."

Pete got in the very rear of the van. As the rest piled in, the duty driver walked around to take the wheel. He frowned at Frankie seated in shotgun.

"Lieutenant, where'd you get these guys?"

"They were out here visiting some old friends."

The driver fastened his seat belt, turned the engine, and looked in the rear view mirror for the rear passengers to cinch up their belts. He saw no action on their part and wasn't about to argue. Unknown to the driver, only three of the old codgers had ever even seen a seat belt. He only noted that they just didn't fit in. The remainder of the ride to Andrews Air Force Base was uneventful and quiet.

Each of the passengers was immersed in his own story and its ending. Tony wondered whether Ruth had moved on, Ricky hoped that his family had forgiven him, Charlie prayed that his folks were okay, and Allan wasn't going to get his hopes up to be let down. Pete prayed that the mission would go well, and that he would make amends with his folks. And Frankie, he didn't have a choice except to heed Tony's words that he could only provide comfort to his widow and little boy. He clenched his teeth in utter despair that he was going to the grave with the song still in his heart.

PETE'S TERROR

The men took advantage of the long flight from the states. The four old timers were productively distracted by the new technology of the aircraft, and also by the new devices that they would use on this mission. An iPhone to them was pure magic when compared to the simple mechanics of the telecommunications of their time. They landed in Kandahar and were transported at dusk to a camp just outside the target in the mountains of Pakistan. As the evening wore on, a crescent moon barely illuminated the war-painted faces of the special team.

Frankie and Pete took charge of the mission plan, and then briefed the others. This was the second bite of the apple for Pete. He realized the challenges, and that one wrong move would be fatal, again. The intensity left absolutely no room for conversation, other than that reserved for the mission.

Each team member sat quietly to reflect on his first death experience. It didn't seem that big of a deal now. Fear of the unknown was no longer an issue for them because they had dealt with it before, and died. They began to associate the pain of their loved ones at that sorrowful time with this mission, but quickly realized that they were clouding their judgment of this night, and what was about to happen.

Pete snapped his fingers to get their attention. He reminded everyone that the next few hours would be their life and warned them not to drift off to another distant dream. Each rogered up and understood that he would have to finish this mission first, and it would have to be performed flawlessly.

After the brief, Frankie and Pete conferred privately.

"Pete, I just want you to know that whatever happens, I would like you to look after my family. You've been my brother during the toughest times and never faltered in being there to comfort and save me, even if it was from me. I realize that you did everything possible to save me from death on the last go around here however, it was my time. As much as I don't believe in hocus pocus, I guess there may be something to it. These old timers surely believe it. If there's one thing that I've learned in the last 24 hours, it's that you consistently do life right, Pete. That being said, you should go back and make amends with your folks."

Pete confessed. "I know that I'm beginning to have an appreciation for everyone in my life, especially those who have suffered from my pig-headedness."

Frankie knew that for all practical purposes his world was over, and he had only this mission and his burial left. All that was left was to walk the pathways of Arlington at night praying for another chance to see Sara and Austin. Those two names would be the hardest words that he would ever speak.

Pete prayed for another chance to make amends at home. He faintly remembered his early years when his mom and he had picnicked in a big field filled with what he thought were white rocks. He wished he could return to those days when he was at peace with her. He couldn't recall closeness with his father, but knew that he had been supportive through his later years at home.

Allan, Charlie, Tony, and Ricky were fidgeting and anxious to get into the fight. They already knew what their dessert would be after this battle. As they waited to move out, Allan and Tony were offering infantry tips to Charlie and Ricky. The closest that Charlie had ever gotten to shooting an enemy was a 50mm anti-aircraft gun in Pearl Harbor. Ricky's experience was strafing from a Phantom F-4 with 20mm weapons at 6,000 rounds per minute, which had certainly offered a greater advantage of survival than a set of boots on the ground. His contribution to the grunts had been dropping napalm, obliterating cover for the enemy. He had been the Cavalry to the ground troops, and they had been thankful.

Tony and Allan were familiar with the danger of ground combat, and shared their tips to create a greater safety margin for the others. Charlie and Ricky were all ears, knowing that they would need every advantage against the enemy. Charlie shared his philosophy that one day in combat for an infantryman was a much greater sacrifice than twenty years of service for someone not in harm's way.

Supplies had been pre-positioned for the group. Tony and Allan found the lighter equipment to be a Godsend compared to the heavy canvas and metal canteens of their time. Light canvas breathable boots took the place of the heavier, leather boondockers. They couldn't believe the new technology of wicking material, and socks that made you feel like you were walking on air. Weapons were much lighter than those carried by the old timers, too. Allan poked the new soldiers' comforts by calling them a bunch of pussies.

The mission was set for 0100 hours, which gave the group about two hours to muster and, with logistics support, to get to the marshal point. The group observed several vehicles moving along a stretch of highway toward a short rising mountain. Pete had taken charge and was greeted along the road by several Special Forces Green Berets. He motioned for the others to join up by the lead truck. The Forward Observers completed a circle for the brief. The Green Beret Captain welcomed the team.

"Good evening gents. My name is Captain Stanley Kosiek. It's a pleasure to meet you. I see we have some seasoned fighters among us."

Pete didn't understand how the Captain knew that the four with them were "seasoned." He blew off the thought and remained on point with the brief, and to hell with the rest.

The Captain smiled at Pete. "We've heard so much about you from our guys."

Again, Pete wondered who their guys were but dropped the notion to inquire.

Captain Kosiek continued. "Our Intel has the bastards holed up in those mountain five clicks ahead. We can't use bunker busters because we want the Intel that's inside. About two weeks ago, another Special Forces team tried to smoke them out and retreated with a casualty."

The others turned their attention to Frankie, who hung his head and looked away.

Pete interrupted. "I'm here to finish this and then get everyone home."

Captain Kosiek spoke again. "Not so quick, Pete. There are many unanswered questions about the trails leading up to the target. You'll have to improvise to make it to the opening. This will take all the skills you can muster, gut instinct, and a great deal of patience. We will have air support with a Walleye LGB on the wing of a Hornet."

Tony raised his hand. "Walleye, LGB, Hornet?"

"Sorry. Walleye is a Laser Guided Bomb, and the F/A-18 Hornet aircraft is the weapons delivery platform. The only way we can get the bomb on target is to have you get close enough to assess the area, move through the vulnerable spots, and put the laser on target. Then we can bring in the air support to link the weapon with the target."

The Captain took his pointer from the front seat of his truck. He drew an oval in the sand to represent the mountain, and with exact replication sketched the area, denoting the possible resisting forces and any barriers to getting into position. In his brief, he mentioned that the last team that moved on this particular target had missed a hidden position of bad guys and had been ambushed. Frankie was reliving every detail because he was the one who had been trapped and caught the unlucky bullet.

Pete remembered it in great detail and had questioned his position to cover Frankie on the assault. Nothing had really changed since their mission here two weeks ago, except that they had four new faces with limited tactical experience in the mountains. Frankie and Pete were brainstorming internally while the Captain continued his brief. They tried to cherry pick the new information out of the pitch while analyzing a strategy other than what they had used the last time.

After the Captain completed the intelligence update, Pete walked over and put his arm around Frankie and moved away from the group.

"I'm telling you, Shipmate, we are going into the same hell but definitely need a different result. If not, then some other poor bastards will follow with another mission into this Al Qaeda prick's central operations hub. This time it's up to us to do it right."

"I can take the lead again, Pete. You can only die once, right?"

"You don't understand. I was sent here for a reason. I was specifically picked to do this. I failed you the last time, Frankie. I have to be successful for these guys . . . so they can go home."

"What?"

Pete snapped back. "No, Frankie! Now I am beginning to understand the choices that you made, and that they made, and why we are all here.

What I haven't figured out is the choices I made. I've got to do this on my terms, my way, and screw it all."

"Are you alright, Pete?"

"Hell yeah. I'm taking the lead when we get there. Frankie, I will need you to take Allan and Tony to provide cover while Charlie and Ricky provide a distraction. I'll work to get close enough to focus the laser once we've determined the most vulnerable point that'll take the bastards out of commission."

Pete broke from the huddle with Frankie to gather the others. He was internalizing his own strategy in hopes that in the end, he would preserve his team. Frankie could sense Pete's concern for the team's safety ahead of his own, but avoided the confrontation with him. Instead, he would personally try to compensate for any mistakes that Pete might make.

Frankie knew how hard-headed Pete was, and unbeknownst to Pete, he had covered for his mistakes in other operations without a word. Frankie thought at times that Pete's bull-headed approach may have been what had cost him his life on the prior assignment. When he thought about it that way, Frankie would get pissed for a moment, but then he would pass it off because that's what you do for a comrade and friend.

Pete was charged up. "Okay, assholes, are you ready to roll?"

You could feel the adrenaline rush and the energy pulsing out of every pore. Their energy was incredible and on a scale of about ten times the rush that football players feel just before a Super Bowl kickoff. After all, this wasn't just a game; it was their lives and ultimately saving the lives of others. All joking had left the group. This was serious business, and Pete's concentration was on the next two hours of the mission. Frankie had never seen Pete so centered in any situation.

"Allan, Tony, when you get to the base of the mountain, there are three pathways leading up to their base operations. Take the one on the left. It will take you slightly above the level of the entrance. Position yourselves where you can get unobstructed shots at any of those turds coming out. Be sure that there are no snipers above your location."

"Charlie, you need to go up the middle, and if you see or hear any movement, take cover, but let them know that you are there. You will distract their attention away from Allan and Tony."

Charlie wasn't too keen on the idea that he was a target for the enemy.

"Ricky, I need you to come in from above and to the right, to serve as another distraction from the main event. Stay covered and provide some shock and awe when necessary."

Ricky had a confused look on his face about the shock and awe reference, but was ready to do his part for his country, again. Then Pete looked at Frankie and smiled.

"This is it, Shipmate. It's my turn to head up the mountain. I need your help to get me up to the center, to the brain. I'll work my way up the middle, with your cover, if necessary, and then, when it's time, you'll need to call in air support to deliver the Walleye to their address. Can't wait to see the Walleye crash through their front window. Are you ready to do this?"

Frankie smiled. "You bet your ass. I owe the bastards big time.

Frankie had to make the offer one more time. "Pete, are you sure that you want to do this? I can deliver the same message without a loss of life."

Pete hugged his brother. "You need to be there in spirit with your family when this is over. You have to see them through the funeral. I owe that to you, and you owe it to them."

Ricky took off up along the ridge, out of sight of the enemy. He was gaining his high hilltop advantage while Allan and Tony crept along the base to the left side of the trail, moving higher into position on the adjacent hill. They were almost in position for their sights to be effective. Charlie ran at full speed to the right side of the hill, keeping cover, ready to distract the adversary should they detect Pete and Frankie moving up the middle. Frankie stayed back about twenty yards to provide cover and observe any bad guys that might detect Pete's presence.

The team stayed engaged, and focused on the mission, ignoring the future. They were100 percent in the present. It seemed that everything was in their favor, with the dimly lit night and slight breeze to muffle their movements. Pete kept a good climbing pace up until he encountered a silhouette in the pathway. He halted his movement and motioned for Frankie to look ahead. Frankie threw up his hands in question, shaking his head east and west. Pete turned to look again, and the silhouette was gone.

Allan and Tony were positioned and loaded for bear. Charlie kept his eye out for cowans who would take offense to the uninvited guest on their front porch. He kept a leading pace to the right side above Pete. Ricky had positioned himself above the cave, and far enough out that he would not be in harm's way of the Walleye. All this time, he had been wishing that he was at the controls of the plane that would be dropping that baby to the guests of honor within the cave.

Pete had recovered from the scare of the silhouette and proceeded on the pathway up. Frankie kept a close eye on his friend and was at the ready to kill any bastard who may try to harm him. They were ahead of schedule and within fifty yards of the set point for the laser. Little by little they made ground and began to question whether anyone was even in there. The only movement now was Pete and Frankie getting closer to the site.

They were within 20 yards of the cave when they saw shadows flickering in the light. Pete saw another silhouette going into the entrance, then an eruption of voices that seemed to be arguing within. Pete took advantage of their distraction; he signaled to Frankie to call in air support, which was about fifty miles out. Immediately, he crawled the final twenty yards, which still kept him out of range of the explosion effects, but close enough to laser the small opening that would beckon the Walleye's arrival.

The plane should have only taken two minutes to be on target, however, it seemed like forever. For some strange reason, two Al Qaeda had emerged in a frenzy from their secluded position, and then began shooting. They had positioned themselves where Tony and Allan couldn't get a shot. Neither Ricky nor Charlie could get a break from the gunfire at Pete. He had to stay in the line of fire to keep the laser on target if they were to be successful.

Frankie crabbed toward Pete in an unsuccessful attempt to provide relief, but he wanted to be close to his friend just in case. Allan and Tony remained engaged with the target, looking for an opening to hit the sweet spot . . . right between their eyes. Ricky dropped a couple of volleys in their vicinity to draw attention away from Pete. Charlie tried to keep pace moving from rock to rock, closer to the target, while trying to maintain a safe distance from any possible collateral damage.

One Al Qaeda soldier turned to see a red laser dot designated on the center, just inside the cave. He scanned the immediate area to locate the source. Pete was becoming impatient for the air cavalry to arrive, knowing that he had only minutes, at the most, before he would be detected. Frankie didn't fire at them because it would draw attention to Pete. He felt completely helpless, but was at the ready to return fire if they sighted his friend.

The enemy fighters visually located Pete in under a minute, leveled their sights in his direction, and began firing. Pete rolled to the side for cover, losing his bead on the target. The American warriors from all sides began to unleash a lead curtain that forced the Al Qaeda to retreat to the cave. After the volley stopped, they could hear the roar of jet engines rolling in. Pete emerged again, out in the open, to laser target the prize. As he put the dot on target, the laser guided bomb released from the ejector racks from the Hornet to find its new home.

Moments before impact, the Al Qaeda began their assault on the intruders. The Americans let loose another barrage of fire to contain them in an effort to keep Pete safe. Within fifteen seconds, the mountain shook violently, fire lit up the sky, and a deafening boom echoed throughout the valley. Heavy shrapnel began falling through the dense cloud of dust, driving all to take cover. Every member of the team had endured the blasts of battle before, but nothing compared to this. Once the initial blast had passed, and they saw that there was no activity in the cave, Allan and Tony rushed to make their way back to the muster point. Ricky waited for a few minutes to provide follow-up fire if needed. He made his way over the ridge and down the hill to meet up with the others. Charlie had plenty of experience with explosions in Pearl Harbor. This event had lacked the water works and the steel projectiles that had penetrated the sailors on the decks of the ships. He headed toward the center trail to catch up with Pete and Frankie.

The air was still and absent of sound. Charlie began to feel in his gut that all was not well. He finally saw Frankie ahead. He was sitting on the ground with Pete in his arms. Charlie felt completely helpless. He couldn't find the words that would make it better. He knew the pain that Frankie was feeling, as Charlie had experienced the same on the *Arizona*. The only difference was that moments after he held his shipmate, he was destined to meet the same fate. For Frankie, it was a reversal of roles. It was he who had been held by Pete just two weeks earlier. There were no words, only a numbness and a hope that all of this pain would quickly go away.

STRENGTH AND HONOR

Pete's parents quietly made their way from the room in the St. Regis Washington D.C. Hotel. The room reservations had been made by the Department of Defense, and the DoD had afforded them any and all assistance that was necessary to comfort them during their trip to the White House. It had been only three months since the loss of their son, and the pain remained intense. It seemed to have taken a huge toll on Arlene, naturally. Kent provided all the attentiveness and sympathy that he could for his wife in order to make the event tolerable.

They were very proud of Pete's courage and valor, but it didn't lend the slightest relief to the pain. Arlene's heart was broken badly, and it showed. They didn't quite know what to expect at the ceremony tomorrow. It was one of those things that you would like to attend but not under the circumstances that had elicited the invitation.

At 1000 hours tomorrow, the President would be awarding the Congressional Medal of Honor, posthumously, to Peter Charles Baker. Kent and Arlene Baker would be there to accept the honors. Kent and Arlene had discussed ad nauseam the what-if's of parenting, and the decisions they had made to guide Pete, but still had no logical conclusion as to how it all turned out the way it did.

The restaurant hostess walked up to accompany them to their seats.

"Miss, can we get a quiet table, please?"

"Yes, Sir."

The hostess sensed the stress and sadness in their actions, and accommodated the request.

"This is semi-private, Sir."

Arlene smiled. "Thank you."

Kent offered Arlene the chair facing away from the crowd. He kissed her on the forehead and took his seat.

"Kent, I know you are sick of the discussion, so can we just quietly sit and eat, please?"

"Yes, Dear."

"Thank you."

The evening went forward as planned in complete silence. The only voices they each heard were their own, in arguments that sought to provide peace within their souls. Once in a while, Arlene would look up and smile at Kent, knowing that he was trying his level best to make her happy. They knew that goal was unachievable, though, and it would take time to return a real smile to her face. They finished moving the food around their plates and ordered the check.

It was early morning when Kent awoke to find Arlene sitting in the easy chair. She was peeking through the curtains at the morning sun, wondering how the day would end. Kent went straight to the bathroom to give her a few more minutes of uninterrupted solitude. She had spent many days since Pete's death stealing minutes of seclusion to dream of the past and elude her present. In what seemed like moments to her, Kent had finished getting ready to meet the day. He went down to get coffee and urged Arlene to prepare for the ceremony.

At 0830, they were picked up by a government car that took them to the security gate at the White House. They held hands tightly, helping each other cope with the imminent pain. Under normal circumstances, a person would look forward to and be impressed with the pomp and circumstance, but on this day they were numb to it all. They wanted to close their eyes and be over it. They were very, very proud of their son, but the hurt was too much to bear.

The couple was escorted to the East Room to meet the President, and get ready for the formality. They were seated on the front row. The Chief of Naval Operations greeted the couple, shared his sincere sympathy for their loss, and then sat down next to them. Several men and officers from Pete's SEAL Team stood at parade rest with their heads bowed. They would not be able to talk to Pete's parents until the ceremony was completed.

Pete's spirit appeared between the Team's formation and his parents. He wanted to run to his mom, grab her up, and take away her agony. He could see how upset she was by the redness of her eyes from the sleepless nights of crying. This wasn't at all what he had planned for his life, especially leaving his folks behind. What had he done? He was thinking that there was no bigger asshole in this world than him. He ran to Arlene, knelt in front of her, wanting to hold her hands, kiss her, console her, but it just wasn't happening. Regardless of how hard he tried, she couldn't see him.

Pete was always fixing things, but now he was powerless to do squat. As he got up, he saw Frankie sitting on the front row at the other end.

"Frankie, what the hell?"

"Pete, you know the drill."

"What?"

"You, like me, have to gut out the pain of the process. They are here because of you. Did you do all you could to ease their pain when you left?"

"You know I didn't."

"Well?"

"How do I fix it?"

"Gut it out, Shipmate. They will get past it. If you remember, I have to go back to be with my family through the process. I also have to come to grips with my death and their future without me."

"I didn't mean to go away mad. I didn't."

"You'd have to be blind not to see the love that your parents have for you, especially your mother."

Arlene sat stoically for the ceremony, which was about to begin. However, she was a broken lady with a severed heart. Her little boy was gone, and everyone in that room knew that was the gospel. The Master of Ceremonies called the group to attention, readying for the memorial honor service to begin.

Kent and Arlene were escorted to the staged area to receive Pete's medal. Pete rushed to his mother's side. The Presenter began.

"The President of the United States of America, authorized by Act of Congress, has awarded in the name of Congress the Medal of Honor to

Petty Officer First Class Peter C. Baker
United States Navy

For conspicuous gallantry and intrepidity at the risk of his life above and beyond the call of duty as the leader of a Special Forces element with Naval Special Warfare Unit Afghanistan on 10 October 2013. While leading a mission to eliminate a Taliban Operational Bunker, Petty Officer Baker demonstrated extraordinary heroism in the face of grave danger."

Pete didn't want it to continue. He didn't want his mother exposed to the painful details. He couldn't stop the words, and had no other choice but to watch this agonizing articulation of his death in front of the lady who had loved him from conception.

The Presenter continued. "Petty Officer Baker continued to engage the enemy until he was mortally wounded, gallantly giving his life for his country and for the cause of freedom. By his selfless leadership, courageous actions, and exceptional devotion to country, he reflected great credit upon himself and upheld the highest traditions of the United States Navy."

The President held the medal out to present it to Kent and Arlene. The room was perfectly still. The President added his personal comments about Pete, but the words fell silent on the group. He could say nothing nor do anything that would bring him back or eliminate the sadness of the situation.

As he finished speaking, Arlene raised her head and wept as she spoke.

"We knew the courage of our son and how extraordinary he was. You knew him for such a short time. I knew him for his entire life. I was blessed for that, and can't imagine how I will ever get past the pain, or if I ever will. I could speak to the many stories of Pete growing up and filling our lives with a lifetime of love, but my lifetime to do so wouldn't be long enough. I do want to thank each of you for being his friend. I know how difficult it must have been for Pete to lose his friend Frankie. We didn't get to talk about it with him, but we know Pete's heart. I can say that my life is over. Pete's is gone."

She became weak and began to tremble uncontrollably. Kent was there to hold her up and guide her back to her chair. It was evident that she hadn't gotten over his death, and probably never would. Pete was devastated and realized that it was too late to make amends. His thoughtless ways of dealing with his parents had finally caught up with him, and his mom was paying his price until the day that she died. She had taken ownership of his leaving the world without even the common courtesy of a loving farewell from him. Pete wanted to crawl in a corner and die, again.

FREE BIRD

Pete's eyes flew open wide. He looked around to see others tightly hugging their jackets for warmth. He shivered from the cold and shook his head hard to gain a perspective of his surroundings.

"This is the Plane Commander. We will be landing at Andrews in thirty minutes."

The Loadmaster walked up to Pete just as the announcement finished.

"Baker, you need to make sure that your transfer case is secured before we land."

Pete hesitated momentarily. "Will do, Sir."

He stood up and looked around. The other passengers were making head calls and prepping for landing. He stretched long and felt pain on the top of his head.

The Loadmaster stopped. "You took a pretty good hit to the head."

"How long have I been out?"

"For almost the entire eight hour flight."

"I'm sorry."

"The corpsman over there checked you out."

The corpsman gave a short salute and smiled. Pete nodded back, and then headed to the cargo area to check on Frankie. He had so many emotions running through his head. He began thinking about his mom and about Frankie, Sara, Austin, and the others in his dream. When he got to the case, his mind focused only on his Charge. Pete ran his hand along the flag draped coffin.

"Frankie. I'm sorry that I didn't check on you till now. You wouldn't believe what I . . . never mind."

Pete looked at the tie downs to ensure that the case's integrity was secure. He patted the case one more time, and then closed his eyes. He asked Frankie for the strength and guidance to help him find the right words for his widow and son, and then he returned to his seat and gathered his thoughts. What would he say to Sara? Would he even try to console her or just hold her while she fell apart? Somehow he was ready to meet reality and deal with it the best he possibly could.

The C-17's gear lowered for final, and then landed at Andrews without event. Pete looked out the window to see what awaited him. He knew now that he would be there for Frankie and those who loved him. The plane taxied off the main runway toward the hangar. Families waited impatiently for their homecoming soldiers; some would walk off, while others would be carried.

The aircraft came to a stop, and the plane captains chocked the wheels while support equipment made its way to plug power into the flying fortress. Pete moved to Frankie's case to walk it out. As the cargo doors opened, the floodlights' beams filled the bay with the illumination of a bright, sunny day. The passengers exited out the front of the aircraft, while the escorts peeked out at the families in the shadows of the trees that hugged the flight line's edge. They could feel the incredible silence of sorrow emanating from the loved ones' hearts. Pete peered at the other escorts' eyes reflecting the torment they were about to face. Their reverence toward the grief-stricken loved ones was second only to their own sadness at the loss of their comrades.

On this particular flight, there was a female Army Sergeant, who had lost her life through gunfire days before. Her escort was a female Army Captain, who had served with her for an entire year in country. She spoke of the Sergeant's incredible bravery, and said that she had a husband and two little children waiting for her at home. Pete noticed a man on the tarmac, standing tall and holding two little children in his arms. What would she say to him?

In addition to the deceased on this flight, there were many who had been maimed, in body and in mind. There were those who were missing one or more limbs, or who had lost their sight. There were some who were badly burned, and then there were those who looked fine on the outside, but were suffering the beginnings of the invisible wounds of Post-Traumatic Stress Disorder (PTSD). Almost everyone who exited the aircraft was a wounded warrior in one way or another.

He could see the tracks of the tears slightly staining their solemn faces, holding it together for the walk down the aft ramp to the hangar. Very few were there to share tears of joy.

The escorts began to walk their fallen friends down the aircraft ramp. Each walked with great timing, clutching their charge's case covered by Old Glory. It would be only minutes before Pete would be meeting with Frankie's family. He could see Frankie's mother and father weak and weeping.

Pete focused on Frankie's son, standing tall, watching the military movements and traditions of returning the honored heroes with the proper protocol. Then Pete, this tough SEAL, almost went to his knees watching Frankie's young bride hold it together. Yes, just as they had rehearsed, she would stand tall, be tough to take on all the heartache that these guys could deliver. They had shared with Pete the importance of Sara's strength in case it ever became necessary to help Austin transition during this type of very difficult time.

Pete spoke to Frankie's spirit. "Okay Buddy, we're on in just a few minutes. Your part is easy from here. And mine, it's going to be a bit tougher. It's been a long flight my friend. I've certainly learned a lot about life, but more about whom and what I want to be. You've been an inspiration for the longest time, and you still keep giving, even though you're not here. I don't think that I could ever do your memory justice, but I will try until it's my turn to go. Ready? Here goes."

Pete walked off the aircraft ahead of the honor guard. He rushed to Sara, and she filled his outstretched arms. Pete planted a big kiss on her cheek.

"This one's from Frankie."

Sara's voiced cracked. "Oh, Pete . . . What are we going to do?"

"We'll just have to make it through the next couple of days together. You have to be tough for Austin. It's what Frankie asked us to do. I'll meet up with you shortly."

Pete walked back to the aircraft to assume his duty as escort. Sara retreated to her parents and Austin, who were standing on the edge of the tarmac. Sara picked Austin up and squeezed him hard.

Austin asked, "Mommy, where is Daddy?"

"We will see him tomorrow, Sweetie. Go with Granny and Gramps. I will see you in a little while."

Sara watched the arrival and transfer ceremony of the cases. She was able to cry now that Austin had gone. After the families had departed, Sara made her way toward the hangar door. The warning buzzer for the closing doors proved to be no deterrent for her as she walked through within full sight of Frankie's transfer case. Pete looked back to see her walk onto the shiny white hangar floors. He quickly shuffled over to her.

"Sara, where are you going?"

"I am going to see Frankie."

"I'm not sure that's possible."

"Stop me. I've waited. I want to see him."

She brushed past Pete in a straight line to her husband.

ALL NIGHTER

This was all new to Pete, being toe to toe with Sara. He waited for some unsolicited intervention from authority, but he was very keen on the point that Sara was mighty strong-willed. He based that knowledge on personal experience and stories from Frankie, and he knew that it would take a major spiritual power to convince her otherwise.

"Sara, I'm not sure if this is okay."

"Pete, I really don't care. I've been away from Frankie for quite a long time, and they aren't moving me from this place."

"Let me at least talk to a supervisor, please? If it were up to me, you could stay forever."

Sergeant Goodwin, the NCO in charge of the unit, observed their exchange and headed toward them.

"May I help you, Ma'am?"

Pete stood silent, knowing that Sara would hold her own.

"I'm Lieutenant Leonardo's wife."

"Yes ma'am?"

She pleaded. "Please, I would like to spend some time with my husband?"

Goodwin, an astute military husband, knew that the only thing tougher than a soldier was his wife. He smiled and conceded to her request. Pete watched the negotiation unfold as he had thought it would.

"Ma'am, you can stay as long as you like. Can we get you a chair?"

"No, thank you. I'll be fine. Would it be okay if I spent the night?"

"It's the least we can do for him, Ma'am. He's done so much for us."

"Yes, he has."

Sara hugged Goodwin and then turned to Pete.

"Pete, tell my folks that I will see them in the morning."

"Okay. I'll be right back."

Pete walked toward the exit door at the side of the hangar. He looked back and smiled. The sergeant motioned to the Corporal standing by the bulkhead.

"Corporal Kinney."

"Yes, Sergeant?"

"Get some things to make a pallet for Mrs. Leonardo. She is our special guest for this evening."

"Roger."

"I'll be right back, Ma'am."

Sara shuffled to Frankie's case, kissed her palm, and placed it gently on the area that she believed would be Frankie's cheek. She stood seemingly dazed for a couple of minutes and then kneeled at the case. Sergeant Goodwin stood by ready to assist her, but respected her personal space with her husband. Corporal Kinney returned with a blanket and pillow from the bunk room. Goodwin reached down and braced his arm inside hers. Sara made her way to her feet so that Kinney could place the blanket next to the transfer case.

"Ma'am, can I get you . . . ?"

She stopped him and smiled. "Thank you."

Kinney's eyes filled as he quickly moved away.

Goodwin asked, "Mrs. Leonardo, is there anything else we can do?"

"No, thank you. I'll be okay."

The Sergeant squeezed her hand with tears welling in his eyes.

"Anytime."

Pete entered the hangar area and looked up to see the young widow kneeling next to her husband. She ran her hand gently back and forth along the red line of the flag at the edge of the transfer case. It seemed like she was trying to summon his spirit. Pete watched her begin a nesting ritual for the evening by fluffing the blankets near the pillow. Pete was amazed at the strength of this young wife, and what she had learned in such a short time of her life with a husband like Frankie.

Her actions may have been instinctive to survival; however, she demonstrated creative power to be in her own world of personal mourning during what she knew would be her last night with Frankie. Pete couldn't bring himself to steal one flick of time from them. He watched the red night-lights illuminate this showcase of intense love and devotion. If ever a picture would remain in Pete's mind, this would be it. This is what he always imagined it should be for a fallen friend and the mate left behind.

The last twenty four hours had been like a cram course on life and death for Pete. He slowly walked toward Frankie and Sara, and then he realized that there was nothing he could say that had any relevance. She was in the moment and so consumed with this night, that she was oblivious to anything or anyone else. Pete retreated to a corner of the hangar where he sat for the remainder of the evening, watching his friend's last farewell, knowing that they would both be at peace come morning.

Sara snuggled close to the case and whispered. "Frankie Leonardo, what are we going to do now? I sent your son home with Mom and Dad. I haven't told him yet. Others think I'm so brave, but I don't know what to say to him. I couldn't bear to break his little heart. This hurts so much, and you're not here to help me. I want you here with me, just like we talked about. This wasn't supposed to happen. Austin won't have you to play with at the beach. How long will it take to make him forget? Will he forget, or will you be with him in all that he does in his life?"

Sara sobbed quietly, hoping that she would hear something from beyond. She had been quiet ever since getting the news from the Casualty Assistance Calls Officer (CACO). Her mind had been on constant rewind and was vivid in every respect about the day that the car pulled up in front of the house. Fortunately, Austin had been in pre-school that morning, which had given her a few hours to adjust before picking him up. Since that time, she had been running quiet, and he sensed something different. Every couple of hours Austin would ask her what was wrong. If she had only told him that day, they would be past the initial pain. However, she was scared to death to break his little innocent heart. She had needed time to figure it all out, but that time had passed.

There isn't a book that's issued to military spouses. There's no instruction on how or when to tell your innocent child that his parent has been killed in action. Each person goes through it on his or her own, and then either regrets their choices or moves on to make the best of it.

Sara asked again. "Frankie, where do we go from here? I have to talk to Austin in the morning on our way to Arlington. I'm sorry that I waited this long. Do you think he already knows? Talking about it won't make it any easier, so, I guess I just need to shape up and move forward."

She nestled her head into the pillow. The intense emotion that Sara had felt throughout the day helped her to drift off to sleep. Frankie's spirit sat on the case and watched her all night long. He was helpless to do anything except pray that she would have his strength now. Pete stood the watch for his friend and wept for the pain that this young widow was enduring. For some reason, his thoughts strayed to his younger days with his own mother.

A MOTHER'S DUTY

Sara's father went to the hangar early in the morning to take her to the Navy Lodge, where he and her mother had spent the night. Pete met him at the flight line gate to allow him access.

"How's she doing, Pete?"

"She slept a few hours. I believe that she found huge comfort being with Frankie last night. She woke up around 4:30 this morning. I kept everyone away so that she could spend the last couple hours alone with him."

When Sara's father walked in, she had already stepped away to the restroom. They waited without words for her return. She emerged and went to her father's embrace.

"How are you doing, kid?"

She hugged him strong. "I'm alright."

"You need to go back to quarters to get cleaned up."

"Did Austin ask for me?"

"No. I think he's smarter than you give him credit for."

"Did he ask about Frankie?"

"Sara, I think it's one of those things that children feel without words."

"I want to take Austin for a walk this morning. Can we go to Arlington a couple of hours early?"

"That's probably a good idea, Honey."

"Pete, would you take us, please?"

"You know I will. I can pick you up at the Navy Lodge. I've got to go to Quarters to get ready. Maybe an hour?"

She hugged his neck and kissed his cheek. "Thanks Pete."

Pete turned over custody of Frankie to the burial detail so he would be available to accommodate her request.

They departed the hangar for lodging. She was trying to capture the right words to say to Austin. Pete was numb from the personal loss of his best friend, and then watching the added emotions that plagued Sara.

Pete arrived at the Navy Lodge at 1000 hours. Sara was patiently waiting outside with Austin. She wore the standard black dress and didn't much care about her appearance. She had always been a naturally gorgeous woman, regardless of time of day or what she was wearing. The only make-up that she owned was a hot red lipstick that made her look sexy to Frankie. Frankie was a very lucky soul. He had hit the jackpot when he found Sara. Pete had always had a little crush on her ever since the first time they had been introduced, but Frankie was totally secure in their relationship. They were deeply devoted to each other and referred to their intense feelings for one another as their "love mojo."

Sara opened the rear door and put the car seat in the back of Pete's rental. Austin knew the drill and jumped to his post, cinching his belt. She leaned over, kissed him, and got in the front.

"Are you ready, Sara?"

"Yep, as ready as I'll ever be."

"Then, on we go."

The ride lasted about 45 minutes in traffic. They were quiet but shared several nervous smiles. Pete was respectful in giving her time to formulate the message that she would have to give to the little rocket man in the back seat. Pete watched her fidget with her hanky and stare into the distance, looking for answers. She remained disengaged in order to work through her plan privately. She was astute enough to know that Pete wouldn't badger her about the pending drama that she really wished would just disappear.

"We're here, Austin."

"Mr. Pete, where are we?"

Pete never expected a Q&A with Austin. Pete quickly looked to Sara for relief.

"We are at the park, Honey."

Pete's lips remained sealed. They didn't have a cemetery pass to the funeral, so they had to park in the guest area. They proceeded past the information counter where Sara excused herself.

"Pete, we're good from here. If you find out what section we are supposed to be at and text it to us, then Austin and I will meet you there."

"Okay. Once I get the coordinates, I will catch up just in case you need me."

"That'd be great."

With incredible intrepidation she struck out with her sidekick in tow. Sara was looking for that special spot. She knew that she would be making many trips to Arlington to see Frankie, so she needed to have that special place where she would find comfort during hard times. She couldn't take Austin to the burial area until she had talked to him. As they walked, Sara noticed a shade tree.

"Let's take a seat in the grass here, Son."

After they sat, she looked at the grave marker. The sun glistened on the carved stone. She almost lost it as she read, "Infant, June 16, 1961, Son of SSgt R J McCann, USAF."

Austin ran his fingers in the stone cuts. "What does that mean, Mommy?"

Now was the time when she would have to tell him that he would never see his daddy again. Her time was up, and she had to come clean now, and Frankie wasn't there to save her.

"It's the place where this man and his son are buried."

"Where's Daddy?"

She took a deep breath, and then began.

"Honey, we are here today to say goodbye to Daddy."

He sat there inquisitively. Her eyes were wide with despair. Austin's silence made it even tougher. There was no door that he would open where she could walk through. She looked to the sky hoping for something to fall, albeit the words wouldn't. Perhaps a limb would put her out of her misery. The floodgates opened and the tears began.

Austin asked, "Daddy's not coming home, is he?"

"No, he's not, Honey. I'm so sorry, so, so sorry."

He looked up, pulled her hands away from her face and said, "Please don't cry, Mommy. It's okay."

Sara held her son hard and cried like never before. She was supposed to be the tough cookie who would help him. Instead, he seemed to make greater sense of it all. Austin pulled his arms out and put them around

Sara's neck, holding on for dear life. They embraced for several minutes. Finally, she pushed him away to find his eyes. She held his shoulders and looked so deeply into her baby's eyes that she could see his soul.

"Daddy died, doing something that he loved with all his heart. He dedicated his life to us, and he dedicated his death to the country that he so believed in. He will always be with us in spirit, always. He didn't want to die. It is just something that can happen while brave people like Daddy are protecting others. People will never know what it's like to die for something until they actually do, and then they can't share that experience."

Austin hung on every word. He looked up intently to hear her next words.

"We have only to believe what he told us before he went away. I listened outside your door that night when he tucked you into bed. You were his buddy, his friend, and no one could ever take your place. We were so very blessed to be loved by him. He was such an incredible human being. There can never be another to take his place in our lives."

She pulled him close.

"Austin, this afternoon we are going to say goodbye to him. Horses will bring him to a spot where his body will stay. From now on, Daddy will always be with us in spirit, in our hearts and minds. Do you understand?"

"I think so. I will miss him a lot."

Exhausted, she gained her balance by holding on to the Infant marker. Just as she got to her feet, Pete walked up. He couldn't believe his eyes. He was speechless. He looked at her, standing beside the marker where Frankie had cried two nights ago, and Pete rolled his eyes.

"What's the matter, Pete?"

"Oh, nothing."

He couldn't explain it, even if he tried.

"We'd better head to the site."

Austin maneuvered between Pete and Sara, and held their hands for the hike over the hill.

Pete glanced in her direction and mouthed the words silently. "Are you okay?"

She responded in the same manner. "Yes."

Pete asked, "How did you end up under that particular tree?"

Confused, she replied, "What tree?"

"The one with the infant marker?"

"I don't know. Why?"

"Never mind."

He knew that there wouldn't be enough time or imagination to have that discussion with her, especially with what was ahead for the day.

21 GUN SALUTE

As the trio crested the hill, they could see that family and friends were milling around the many graves. They were passing time reading the names of the many heroes and veterans; the permanent residents of Arlington. They each wondered if others in the future would see Frankie's gravestone and wonder who he had been. They would read the names and try to put a life with each one. There was so much history of relationships and stories that lie just feet below the green grass. Who were they, and to whom did they belong? How many years have to pass before familiar faces no longer come to continue the personal connection? When do strangers take their places?

The fields of white stone were pretty this time of year. Volunteers had come a week earlier to place small American flags on every marker, just like they did every Memorial Day to signify that they remember the service to country rendered by the heroes buried there.

Today was unlike any other visit that Pete had made to Arlington. For some reason, he recalled a familiarity of sorts, and it wasn't one of his visits to see Audie Murphy's grave. He brushed it off as part of his dream, shook his head, and came back to the present.

Sara touched his shoulder. "Are you okay, Pete?"

"Oh, sorry."

They continued walking to the burial site. Pete broke formation to talk with the Ceremonial Guard because he had been asked to present the flag to Sara. It was an agreement that he and Frankie had made long ago in BUDS training. Sara met up with her parents and then went to greet Frankie's parents, who had just pulled up. The Honor Guard asked Pete to assemble the family and friends to begin the ceremony. A couple of Marines ushered stragglers onto the site.

Everyone took his or her seat, and with impeccable timing, the Caisson made its way over the hill toward the site. There was a stillness that invaded the air and seemed to steal the sound from it all. It was hard to catch a breath while the shivers of heartache emanated from within. Sara's parents settled in behind her, giving way for Frankie's parents to have the front row. Sara's mother rested her hand on her daughter's trembling shoulder.

It seemed rather uncanny that this young widow would know the protocol for an event that she had never experienced before. Her composure was probably more fatigue induced than defined by internal control, though.

Austin tapped her hand. "Mommy?"

"Shhh. We can talk later."

Her mind was mush. Her body was numb from any further pain. All eyes were on the detail as they carried the coffin toward the grave. Sara began to show the first signs of coming out of shock, and she was beginning to understand the full impact and meaning of what was happening. She trembled as the salty taste of tears saturated her lips. She became deaf to the words that were being spoken. The scene before her was just a murmur, with the slow motion of bodies passing in front of her. Then a voice reached inside her head. Pete was kneeling before her at eye level. Her empty eyes met his. His hands were shaking.

"On behalf of the President of the United States, the United States Navy, and a grateful nation, please accept this flag as a symbol of our appreciation for your loved one's honorable and faithful service."

He laid the flag on her lap, and she mustered a faint smile. Pete returned her smile with a wink and a wet cheek. He did a right-face and marched to the end of the seating area. All eyes were on Pete while he did an about-face in the direction of the Honor Guard.

The Honor Guard Commander ordered, "Ready, Aim, Fire."

Sara jumped out of her skin at each of the three rounds. Maybe it was the synchronized firing of seven guns that compounded the effect, or maybe it was that she just wasn't mentally engaged in the event.

"Reset. Present Arms."

Taps followed the Commander's orders. Everyone knew that this was the end. It was the final farewell to a loved one, a friend, and anyone who had honorably served his or her country. Silence followed with the gradual movement of the immediate family to the casket. Frankie's parents stood next to Pete. Sara's father scooped up Austin, while her mother took Sara's arm to join Frankie's family.

People began walking the receiving line, offering condolences and hope to the family. There was only a limited number of Frankie's SEAL Team there. Most of them were still in Afghanistan debriefing. The finale of the ceremony would become reality pretty quickly, and then it would be the immediate family who would offer their love and respects to Frankie.

Sara's father and mother were up to say goodbye, with Frankie's parents in tow. Pete walked close behind Sara and Austin. He felt that's what Frankie would have wanted. Now that Frankie was gone, it was up to Pete to help them through the tough times. Sara moved slowly, in hopes that staying with him would last forever. But reality had set in, and she needed to toughen up for the little recruit. She wanted to be a little selfish since this would be her last goodbye to her sailor.

She motioned for Pete to go ahead. "I want to be the last to say goodbye."

"Absolutely."

Pete stood over the casket. "Frankie, I love you, Shipmate. I'll keep a watchful eye on them for you. No need to worry, pal."

He smiled and walked a short distance to allow her privacy.

Sara led Austin forward. "Austin, we'll be back, so just say so long to Daddy."

Austin had watched the others walk past the casket, speak, and drop a rose. He wouldn't be outdone so he followed suit and then patted the top.

He whispered. "Daddy, I'll be back, okay?"

Austin found his way over to the caisson to pat the horses. She watched to make sure that her folks were looking out for his safety, and then proceeded to the casket. She knelt, placing her cheek to his.

She began to whisper. "I'm glad that I spent time with you last night, sailor. You would be proud that I remembered what you taught me. Red at night, sailor's delight. It was my delight to be alone with you just one more time. I never signed up to leave you here by yourself."

She hesitated, wiped the tears, and began again. "Who will take care of you now? Yes, you're tough enough, but you still need me to keep you ship-shape, Honey. I'm glad you gave me this little boy, and I'm not angry with you. Did you know that you would be leaving? I'm so sorry for everyone like me today, but I'm sorrier for everyone like you."

Pete stood waiting patiently for her to finish. He scanned the perimeter and noticed the six pallbearers leaving. They turned to wave at him. He thought he recognized four of the six. He rubbed his eyes and looked again. It looked like Allan, Charlie, Tony, and Ricky. They smiled and kept walking. He couldn't pursue them. He had to remain here.

Sara offered her final farewell just as she had when they were about to go to sleep on the night before he left for his final mission. "Sleep tight and don't let the bed bugs bite. Sweet dreams, Sweetie."

She called to Pete. "I'm ready."

He asked, "Are we heading back to the hotel?"

"Nope."

He was happy to see her smile. The mood began to pick up.

"Where to, little lady?"

"Frankie always said that if anything should ever happen to him, we should gather up friends and family and head to the Pour House. It a Gator's safe house. He said that we should celebrate his life."

Pete quickly replied. "I'll tell the others from the group, and then we can head out. Frankie was obsessed with those damn Gators. Do you think that his folks would go?"

She smiled. "Hell yeah, they will. They'll want to hear all the stories, and so would I. He can't stop them now."

They caught up to the group and gave directions. Austin left with the grandparents, and Pete and Sara walked back through the cemetery to the guest parking. They passed the spot where she had stopped to talk to Austin. Pete stopped and grabbed her arm. "How did you come to stop here?"

"I just did. I don't know. Why?"

He shrugged his shoulders and pointed to suggest that they get a move on. He couldn't explain how he knew that the tree was there from a dream he had had forty eight hours earlier. He wanted to sort it out after she was gone, and when he had a clearer mind.

GHOSTS FROM KOREA

Pete had driven about ten minutes out of Arlington and was fiddling with the radio to find something that would change the mood from pain to party. He had a rental car on which the dials had been pre-set to all the religious and talk show stations. He tired of the effort and shut it down. Sara leaned against the passenger door trying to give relief to her strained back from the tension of the times.

She looked his way. "I can't believe we are here without our buddy. It seems so strange."

"I definitely know that."

They had ridden a bit further without conversation when Pete turned the wheel to exit the interstate.

"The bar is that way, Pete. "Where you going?"

"I need to make a stop."

"Where?"

"I need a fix my lady, and my drug of choice is on the way to the bar, if we take the long way."

"And that might be?"

He placed his index finger to his lips. "Shhh."

He passed the Jefferson Memorial transiting toward the Mall. He pulled into the first parking spot.

"Where are we?"

They exited the car, Pete gripped her hand, and they headed for the Vietnam Memorial Wall. He then took a hard right. He stayed well ahead of her pace, almost dragging her. His pace slowed as the Korean War Memorial came into view. The sun had begun to set, but the air was still the perfect temperature to be comfortable. They walked to the edge of the field to a bench facing the soldier statues. They sat quietly, holding hands, while looking out across the monument field.

"Do you know what this is, Sara?"

"No."

"This is the Korean War Memorial."

"Oh."

He tried to add a little levity to the afternoon in his Elmer Fudd voice. "Be vewy, vewy quiet."

They sat there looking at the stone faces of the statues, each wondering if any of the statues resembled a real person. It hadn't been until today that they both had actually understood that heroes were real people. They had finally learned today to share the pain that loved ones feel when the guys like the men depicted in these statues never returned.

Pete exclaimed, "This is my most favorite place, ever! This is special to me. Just look at those guys! They look like they are walking right at us, begging our help to get them outta there. They're scared, tired, lonely, and in a state of total hopelessness. Can you see the sadness in their eyes?"

She got up and walked as close as she could without crossing the chain. "Yes, I think I do."

He continued. "It's these men that bring me here. It's what inspired me to become a Navy SEAL. I wondered what it would be like to trade places with these fellas so that they could go home to their families. Wouldn't that be a treat for them? I would do it, you know. Think I'm nuts?"

She touched his cheek. "Not at all. I think that's how Frankie felt, too, but he never really opened up when it came to sensitive kind of stuff. He was always the tough, John Wayne type."

"I think it's how we're built. I've never had anyone to share this with before. Maybe it's just a lot of emotion built up, especially losing Frankie, but I never really understood what I was feeling until the last few days. It hit me while watching you at the ceremony. I put Frankie's face on these guys and realized that he is where they are now, and I can't help him. Like I said earlier, I would rather be here standing all day so that he could be sitting here with you. That would make this statue smile. Sara gripped Pete's hand and cried.

She sighed. "We played hard most of the time because I guess; deep down inside we knew that this day might come."

"I felt a little driven here by Frankie to explain the pain that we feel for all the fallen who came before us. I believe that there are others out there now who will take care of Frankie. Unlike Frankie, I only had my folks to worry about, and I thought that if I kept them at a distance, the hurt wouldn't be as bad if I didn't return."

"That's silly, Pete. As your friend, I am begging you to help them and help yourself by making amends. Haven't you learned anything from watching your friends leave this world with loose ends?"

"I have already planned on going home next week. The last couple of days have cured me of having a life without closure."

"Good. Your mom will be elated, and you will feel greater peace within."

"Hey. I'm supposed to be here for you, Sara. It seems as if I'm getting the life lesson from you."

"I learn every day. Frankie used to cite John Wayne, who said, "Life it tough, and it's even tougher when you're stupid.""

"I don't want to fight my parents. I realize now how much they truly love me."

She pointed to her watch. "We'd better skedaddle. They'll have the police looking for us."

They jumped up and turned to go. Sara reached for a hug, and Pete complied. He turned and saluted his stationary friends, then departed not far behind her.

THE POUR HOUSE

T he Pour House was the Gator Nation's refuge in D.C. Spirits there were always high, regardless of whose jersey you wore through the door. The cheers of like-minded fans usually greeted you whenever you entered. Today was quite different, though. Masses of folks who had known Lt. Leonardo had gathered in the center to claim their circle of cheer. Local military veterans watched with delight as the uniforms filled their haunt.

Sara's folks were getting a little worried that something had happened to her and Pete. They sat at a high top table with Frankie's parents and waited. Frankie's father settled for small talk but inside was chomping at the bit to express his terrible loss and great love for his son. He was not distracted by the loud patrons and remained focused on what he wanted to say to the crowd.

Pete and Sara could hear the cheers and music from a block away. They had agreed to celebrate Frankie's life and what he had represented. Over the last few days, their sorrow meters had pegged out. It was enough pain for a lifetime. They knew that Frankie would have honored another shipmate's death by sharing the greatness that he or she had represented in life.

Pete swung the door open like John Wayne in a Western saloon. Cheers rose from every corner. Patrons knew the cause of the celebration and together they became ground zero for honoring one life, that of Lt. Frankie Leonardo. Within the last hour, the emotions had swung from despair to delight. Certainly, the latter mood would carry uplifting stories of an honorable father, husband, warrior, and son.

Fellow SEALS rushed over to greet Pete and Sara with shots and smiles. Sara was so proud that to a person, each SEAL was there to honor his friend and support the family. Frankie would have been so proud. She made her way through the epicenter of the gathering to her parents and Frankie's parents. They were pleased to see that she was in a better frame of mind; however, they knew the pain that she carried deep inside her heart. She hugged each one and thanked them for being there. She wanted to make sure that they were okay with the celebration. Like her, Frankie had shared his philosophy of "celebration upon death" with his parents a couple of missions ago.

Mr. Leonardo couldn't wait any longer. He had to share his feelings about his son with everyone.

"Can I have your attention please?"

An astute SEAL not far away saw his attempt to get the crowd's attention and shouted, "Attention on deck! Lieutenant Leonardo's father has the floor!"

The bar went quiet immediately. Frankie's dad raised his glass, glanced at his wife, and stopped. This was going to be pretty tough for a man who used to play with his son, just as Frankie had with his. Everyone in the bar understood and waited a time for him to gain his composure. He had memorized what he wanted to say but hadn't thought of the emotion that was now blocking his way. Tears ran down his cheeks, and his chest quaked with unprecedented feeling.

He smiled at his wife, took a deep breath, and began.

"First, I can't thank you enough for being here today; for us but mostly for Frankie. I know that if my son were here today, he would be leading the charge to toast a friend. I never imagined in the twenty-seven years that I've known my son, that I would be saying farewell to him. A parent is supposed to leave this earth first. I've never seen such a testament of fellowship, so genuine, so deep, in my life. I can't find words that are worthy enough for you all. Please accept my family's thanks for your support, your friendship, and for something that Frankie believed in so much that he gave his life for, your patriotism for the United States of America."

Sara raised her glass. "Hear, hear, Dad."

The crowd responded. "Hear, hear!"

They rose to their feet, lifted their cheer, and applauded Mr. Leonardo.

Frankie's SEAL Team brothers were a very respectful bunch. They realized that the last two weeks of the tragedy had overwhelmed the family both physically and mentally. They paid their respects to the families and offered their unconditional support at any time and any place, and then these fine comrades retired to the base club where they could quietly share their emotion with each other and have base comrades look out for their safety getting back to Quarters.

Pete and Sara exited the bar shortly after midnight. Her parents waited at the corner for her to say good night to Pete. The neon sign cast its long, dark shadows into the night.

"Thanks Pete. Thank you for being here. Thanks for bringing Frankie home. I will never forget this day, and that you were here for me, for Austin, and for your friend."

"Sara, if the tables were turned, Frankie would have done the same, except better."

He smiled.

She replied. "You need to think about how Frankie would have dealt with your folks."

"I know. Lecture time is over, teacher. My first trip will be home to square away my issues."

"I knew you would see it my way."

He smiled. "You are a pretty resilient lady. You have endured the worst and still have time to fix others. I promise I will go home."

She wagged her finger at him. "You'd better, or I'll kick your ass."

With that, Pete grabbed her and held her as tightly as he could without hurting her.

"You'd better go. Mom and Dad are waiting."

"Pete, can I call you sometime?"

"Call me anytime, Sweetheart. I will always be there for you and the little guy."

FAMILY

Arlene was dealing with the excitement of her son coming home today and the anxiety of what would happen during his visit. The last time he left home, she had cried for weeks. They had argued about his going into the Navy rather than attending college. She had already heard the news of Frankie's death, and she felt incredible guilt that she was relieved that it was someone other than Pete. She had run on nerves all day prepping for his arrival.

Kent and Arlene hadn't seen him in more than two years. They would get the obligatory seasonal cards, and if they were lucky, a call when he was being deployed to another secret location. They often prayed for his safe return as a minimum. More than that would be a bonus. Kent would be home from work in a few minutes, which was always a good distraction for Arlene from her usual pity party.

She was putting the finishing touches on dinner when she heard Kent dragging in the garbage cans from the curb.

He entered the kitchen. "Babe, have you heard anything from your son?"

She wrung her hands in the way she usually did when she was nervous. Kent grabbed them and placed them around his waist. He always broke that chain of worry by way of a warming embrace.

He asked again. "Well, did you?"

"No, I haven't heard anything. I was hoping that he would have called on his way here."

Pete passed Mount Trashmore and smiled. Mount Trashmore was originally a dump about seven miles out of the city limits of Virginia Beach. It had been transformed into a park for the city. His mom and dad would take him there on the weekend to fly kites and have picnics. He had

110

spent the better part of his three hour trip from D.C. thinking about what he would say to them. It would be his transition from rotten kid to good son. What he had to say would be better said in person.

Kent made his famous Rumba drink, which consisted of two jiggers of Sailor Jerry spiced rum, and an equal amount of passion fruit juice. That was the secret formula to help ease Arlene's nerves. He served it up at the kitchen island where she was making a Caesar salad.

He held it out to her with a smile. "What do you think?"

She took a gulp. "That's just what I needed."

He looked at her and laughed. "I meant, what do you think the visit will bring this time?"

"Oh, I really don't know. I just thank God that he's not the one staying at Arlington."

"Yeah, at least he's coming home. That, my love, is a start."

She smiled and patted him on his heart. "You are a good man, Mr. Baker."

Kent had always been there for Arlene and Pete. He was a warrior in his own right. He fought the fight every day, even though it was never on the battlefield. Without hesitation, he had always been there to quell arguments and make everything better. The battle over Pete's going to college was the only time he had been defeated. He just couldn't fix Pete's way of thinking, nor could he explain to Pete why he and Arlene felt so strongly about the argument.

Arlene jumped when she heard a car door slam in the driveway. They could see through the curtains that it was Pete. He was pulling his bag out of the trunk, and then he put it back. He looked relaxed and smiling.

Arlene looked at Kent. "He's a handsome young man."

They heard a long overdue voice from the past nearing the back door.

"Hey, is anybody home?"

Arlene dropped her towel on the counter and ran to the door. She was reeling with excitement to see him. She had waited and suffered so long just for the chance to hold him again. Pete scaled the stairs in one step. Arlene hit the door as he pulled the screen door handle, and in a virtual tie they swung the door open, breaking the chain, and hitting the side of the house. Kent stood tall and choked up at the sight of the reunion.

Pete grabbed her in his arms, reached around her mid-body, and swung her like a school girl.

"Mom, I've missed you so much."

She sighed and broke into tears. She didn't want answers. She was thrilled just to have him in her arms. It was reminiscent of the scared little boy who used to run to her in his childhood. Kent couldn't hold back the tears. He reached out and joined the hug fest.

She found words through her emotion. "Honey, I can't tell you . . ."

Pete would not let go. "Mom, Dad, we need to talk. I've been to hell and back in the last couple weeks. I've seen more pain than you can imagine."

Kent tried to ascertain whether Pete was describing a revelation or having a meltdown.

He offered. "Let's sit and have dinner. We can talk there. Mom's really put on the dog. She worked for two days making your favorite roast. We're so pleased that you're home, Son."

"Can I help you do anything, Mom?"

"No, just take a seat and enjoy. I'll be right back."

Kent knew where she was. She had gone to her bedroom to dump two years of not knowing whether this day would ever come.

"Where did Mom go?"

"She'll be back shortly. The past two years have caught up with her."

"Is she okay?"

"She is now. Thanks, Pete."

He felt like a thug because of his past behavior, but he understood and respected her time to cry.

Kent and Pete went to their old, designated seats, which had been appointed years earlier. Pete scanned the rooms from his vantage point to see what changes had been made in the homestead. Kent was straightening his napkin and utensils to conform to his OCD.

Pete smiled and asked, "Dad, why didn't I inherit that trait from you?"

"It was challenging for me to learn organizational skills in the Navy, but I'll bet I can give you a run for your money now."

Arlene emerged from the kitchen with a basket of her homemade biscuits. Pete couldn't wait to dive into them with a slab of butter.

She sat down and began passing the food. "C'mon, dig in boys before it gets cold."

Pete felt the comfort that he had missed for so long. He had been beating himself up internally until today. This day would be his time to make it different from now until the end of time.

Arlene broke the silence. "I'm so sorry about Frankie. How did everything go last week?"

"Mom, if you guys don't mind, I'd rather talk about that later. Right now I just want to sit and enjoy us and discover."

Kent had to ask. "Discover what?"

"You know, what others have in their lives, or like what Frankie lost."

They sat quietly making their way through the meal. Kent and Arlene waited for Pete to finish, watching his every move. They could see that he was out there somewhere in his mind, thinking.

Pete looked up. "I've had an interesting few days. Right in front of my very eyes I watched the life leave my best friend's body, and I've met so many others who never got to finish their lives; lives that they wanted to finish. I feel like I've died and come back a better person for the experience. It took all of that to help me understand."

His parents were baffled by the comments, and it showed in their expressions.

"I had to lose to gain."

Kent touched his hand. "Pete."

"Please let me finish."

He leaned back in his chair and gestured a polish salute.

"I'm sorry. I'm doing it again. I made it all about me. Go ahead Dad."

"We felt like we lost you a long time ago, Pete. The day you left, we didn't know whether you would ever come home again, dead or alive. You see, we do understand about losing someone. I'll let your mom tell you."

Arlene was content not to engage in further conversation because it was beginning to sound like so many of the talks before. She surely didn't want to digress to the point where Pete would leave again.

Kent reached out his hand to hold Arlene's. "It's okay. Tell him."

She didn't understand what he was trying to get her to say.

"Arlene?"

Pete became agitated. "Tell me what?"

She fumbled her fork to the floor and leaned to the side to pick it up, but she left it there and pulled her napkin to her face as the tears began to run down her face.

"Mom, what's going on?"

She couldn't speak. Pete got up and walked over to console her. She stood and hugged his neck, but he wasn't getting any answers. She turned and went to the living room, wondering how she could articulate the great lie into something that wouldn't end up in another one of Pete's ugly departures. She moved to the sofa and signaled for him to sit next to her. Kent stood up and leaned in the doorway that was the room's entrance.

Pete waited for Arlene to compose herself. He held her trembling hands, watching her intently, waiting for something.

With a crackly voice she began. "Son, we understood exactly what you were doing when you left home."

She looked to Kent for support. He nodded his approval. She knew that it was up to her to tell the story. Pete adjusted himself, sitting farther back in the couch.

Pete asked, "How's that, Mom?"

"Well . . ."

"Mom, I came here to let you know that I get it now. That's it. That's all I really wanted to say."

Kent interrupted. "Let your mom finish. This is about your life, and it will help you better understand."

"Understand what?"

Pete looked at his mom and inquisitively tucked his chin in.

Again she began to explain. "The reason we understood, the reason we were so dead set on your going to college and not to war, was that we had already lived through it once."

Pete was growing impatient to know what she was talking about, but he gave them time for explanation.

"I should have told you before now . . . that I had already lived through it once with your father."

Pete's eyes stared straight at Kent.

She pulled his chin back to look at her. "Your father went away and left us. He was hell-bent on leaving for a better cause. He never came back."

Pete turned his head again in Kent's direction. "What?"

She continued. "I was so afraid that it would happen to me again, but this time it would be my son. I tried to explain before you left the last time, but you wouldn't listen."

She wasn't giving Pete any openings for comment. Tears kept coming. Pete looked at Kent and then back to his mom.

"You see, Pete. I had already gone through what Sara is going through now. You, Pete, were the little boy, and I was the young widow."

Pete looked at Kent. "So, you're not my real father?"

Kent deferred to Arlene for the answers.

She smiled at Kent and responded. "This man has been everything to us ever since your real father died. He has been honorable and a good provider for our entire marriage. You were three years old when Kent entered our lives."

Pete sat silently, taking in the words, and very much surprised by what was unfolding before him. He thought he had heard and seen it all in the last two weeks, but this was the chart topper.

She began. "Andrew, your real father, and I met at the end of our senior year in high school. We spent the summer at the beach and fell in love. Summer was over, and I was going away to college at William and Mary. Your father's folks could only afford for him to attend Tidewater Community College. For the first couple of months, on weekends we would meet at Dam Neck beach. I ended up getting pregnant around Thanksgiving, and life for us changed."

"I couldn't stay in college, and I came back to Virginia Beach. We quickly figured out that because of the baby, we had greater responsibility and needed to plan our future. We used to go to the beach at night where we watched the SEALS train in the moonlight. Those guys were mystical to Andrew, and stirred his interest to become one."

"When I came home for Christmas break, we were supposed to talk about our future. Instead, he had already enlisted and would leave for Basic in February. It wasn't long before he was selected for Army Special Forces training, which meant, as you know, that we rarely saw each other. You were born in June, and shortly thereafter we went to visit him after training."

Pete interrupted. "Sara and Austin came out to visit Frankie after training, too."

She smiled. "I know. There are a lot of parallels, which you shared about Frankie and Sara, which kept the past alive and real for me."

Arlene shared a time when she and Pete had been at Arlington. He had been three years old, sitting on the front row of the memorial service. The gunfire shook her to the very core in her recall, as it had when they were there.

"Son, we were there on the front row of life. The Honor Guard lifting the flag, folding it, and then handing to us. That was my time just as it was Sara's time last week. I vowed never to be there again, so when you wanted to leave, my memories began to roll on an endless loop, playing over and over again. You and I were there, left all alone to wonder what would become of us. After that, we would drive to Arlington every Sunday to visit your father. We picnicked and played, hoping that we would find answers."

Pete realized then where his familiarity with Arlington had come from. "Mom, I remember."

She continued. "Then, six months later, a wonderful man appeared. You have known him to be your father until this very day. Kent could see the pain in my heart, and he saw this precious little boy and knew that he would need the guidance of a good man. From that day forward, he's done all the right things. He was a blessing to us, and he has always respected the special history that we once had with your real father. He has never wavered in support for me or you. I would like to think that Andrew, your dad, would have approved of my choices."

"Mom, I know exactly what you're talking about. All of those who died and never got to go home. They only wanted the best things for those they left behind. I do understand. I'm so sorry, Mom. I wish I had known."

"Son, it's probably the biggest mistake of my life. I should have told you years ago."

He slid closer to her. They hugged and cried.

Pete consoled her with his words. "Mom, I'm proud of my heritage, and I'm proud of you and especially this man who raised me. If I were King for a day, I would ensure that all of the fallen soldiers that I know would have had their families taken care of by someone like him."

His words confused Kent and Arlene. How would he know fallen soldiers?

"You did well, both of you. You were handed a pile of caca and gave us all a wonderful life. I couldn't have asked for more."

The moving exchange caused Kent to leave the room and catch some air. In his heart, he knew well that he had always done the right thing, and this was the validation that he waited so long to witness. A smile crept over Kent's face as if this were a gift to both him and Andrew. Arlene found a peace that she hadn't known in years. She looked up and smiled, and she knew in her heart that things had turned out as they should.

HATE TO GO

The smell of bacon and French toast made its way to Pete's bedroom. He stretched out and enjoyed the pleasure of his old bed without the hustle and bustle of the mission. He rolled over to the nightstand to catch one more glimpse of his real dad. Arlene had given him a photo the night before. He favored his father in his build and facial characteristics. The fact that the photo showed his dad in uniform made him look even that much more familiar.

He couldn't stand the wait. "Mom, is breakfast ready?"

She smiled as she walked toward his door. "You'd better get out here before I feed it to the dogs."

He knew better than that. Their last dog had torn up the house pretty bad. Pete swore that she had had that one put down after he joined the Navy.

"Do I have time for a shower?"

"Sure."

She always gave in to Pete. Kent used to say that she was going to raise a sissy. He called that one wrong. Arlene had the table set and everything covered waiting for her brat to make his presence at the table. As always, she was patient and smiling. Pete's grin preceded his presence as he made his way to the table. He sat in the chair adjacent to Arlene to be close.

"Hey Mumsy."

"How'd you sleep?"

"Like a dead man."

"Really?"

He lifted the cover from the casserole. "I could eat a cow."

"Sorry, no cow, only hog this morning."

He smiled and patted her hand. His whole demeanor had gone one-eighty out. Arlene had asked him about his tour, and what was in his future with the SEALS. As she expected, he was vague with the responses. He consumed enough breakfast to feed three men, and Arlene was content just to watch the love of her life savor her cooking, and then just enjoying him while he was there.

"What time do you have to leave?"

"I don't have to be back until tomorrow, but I wanted to stop by Arlington to visit Dad's grave."

It pleased her to know that she had raised such a fine young man. She would like to have gone with him, just like old times, but she would wait for another time to be asked. After all, she didn't want Kent to feel abandoned with the newfound dynamics in the relationship. They finished the dishes together and talked about future visits. She didn't want today to end. She had the truth out in the open, and this new calm was refreshing, especially the peace within Pete.

Pete returned from his bedroom with his bag and the framed photo that she had given him the night before.

"Mom, can I keep this?"

"It always belonged to you."

"Thanks."

He walked to the car and threw his bag in the back seat of his rental. Arlene hung close to her boy. She was feeding off his positive energy and wanted to take in as much as possible before he departed for places unknown.

"Is Dad coming home?"

"He couldn't break away, but asked me to wish you well."

She believed that Kent had wanted them to have private time and had stayed away intentionally.

"You know, I feel an even greater bond with him knowing that he took on a family not of his making."

"That's a great way to look at it, Pete. You really had two fathers give their lives for us. I know that I loved them both, and I feel that they each had their own special qualities that added to our lives. One made you, and the other protected you."

"I agree Mom. I've really got to roll so I can make it to Arlington before dark."

"You make sure . . ."

"I know, wash my face brush my teeth, wipe my . . ."

"Keep it clean, young man."

"That's what I'm talking about, Mom."

Arlene would always tilt her head back to keep the tears in her eyes and off of her cheeks. Pete would tilt her head forward to let them flow.

He then looked into his mom's eyes.

"Mom, you are spectacular. You made all the right decisions. Andrew made the right choice for you to be his wife, even if only for a short time. This living dad that I have now is the greatest for so many reasons. I believe that Andrew would enjoy slamming beers with him. That's till it was time to go home. Who do you think would win your favor to go home with at the end of the night?"

"Pete, that's for me to know, and you to never mind. Although, it might be fun to have two guys fight over this old broad."

"I would."

"My next wish it that you find someone to make you happy."

"That's a long way off, but when it happens, I want someone just like you. Of course, a little younger like Sara. It's funny how history repeated itself. Sara and Austin are just a twenty-year-younger version of us. I promised Frankie that I would check on them from time to time. She promised to keep in touch with me until they get through this."

"That's kind of you, Pete. Right after your father died, we had the support of the Navy Wives, but then they went on with their transfers, missions, and the list goes on. Then we were on our own. The two of us, just like peas and carrots."

He smiled with her movie reference. It was a game that they had played when he was growing up.

She grinned big. "Life has been great, and it keeps getting better."

Pete added. "Life began making a turn for me when we were at the White House."

"You were at the White House?"

"Mom, that's a long story for another time. Got to get going Jen-nee. I'm meeting Lieutenant Dan at Arlington today."

She dope slapped him. He smiled, picked her up, and kissed her cheek. "Love you, Mom."

Pete got in the car, rolled down the window, and reached out for one more touch.

"Please tell Dad I said thank you. I'll call you this evening."

Her day was complete. She walked toward the edge of the street to wave until he was out of view. Halfway down the street, Pete got out of his car and threw a big kiss. She waved him off and laughed.

REFLECTIONS

I t was Frankie's first night among the spirits at Arlington as one of their permanent party. He was still stinging from the burial yesterday. With all the forewarning from the others, he still ached to be with his family. It was quite a walk from his coordinates to where he thought the group would be meeting, so he stopped and asked some comrades if they had seen the four fighters who had just returned from the Afghanistan mission. They told him that they would be mustering around midnight in front of Lee's House atop the hill, which overlooked the city.

Charlie, Tony, Ricky, and Allan sat on the lawn in front of the house and shared their guesses and hopes for what awaited them in their old lives. Frankie arrived before they began discussing their expectations.

He smiled for their newfound prospective treasures of homecoming, but he was dying inside that he wouldn't be joining them.

"Hey guys. Howgozit?"

They answered in concert. "Great, Frankie boy! Howgozit with you?"

"I made it past the burial. It hurt so badly to watch all the raw emotion."

Charlie replied. "It doesn't get any easier as time goes by."

He might as well have taken a spear to Frankie's soul.

Frankie mumbled. "I guessed it wouldn't."

Charlie was sorry for the hurtful words.

Frankie quickly changed the subject.

"So what time do you all take off?"

Allan was quick to reply. "Not soon enough."

Charlie spoke up. "I'm not sure what I'll find. It's been seventy years since I left, so that would make my sister eighty four. My folks, well they would be well over one hundred. I don't think that I should have taken a slot that someone else could have used."

For a moment Frankie thought that he might get the offer to take his place, but he knew the rules were in cement from the top. JFK and Audie had been clear on that. It wasn't his time yet.

Charlie was thinking about the time he had missed with his folks. His thoughts went back to that last afternoon barbeque. He smiled and truly didn't want to give up hope. He had lived to write letters and share his life in the Navy, and they had loved reading his stories and lived vicariously in the foreign ports and exotic lands by his travels. He had always taken them away, in spirit to a better place. He felt badly that Helen had lived in his shadow, but he knew that she had loved and admired him. In his rather short time on earth, he had brought a lifetime of joy to them, and that was what he tried to believe in his heart.

Tony chimed in. "Isn't anything stopping me now. I'm going back, come hell or high water, even if it's to find Ruthie with another man. I've been dreaming about this for decades. If she's with another man, I'll kick his ass out and take up right where we left off."

Ricky smiled. "Hey, tough guy. You're 28, and he's maybe 90. Do you think it would be a fair fight?"

"Maybe you have a point. Either way, I've been waiting on the hillside in Normandy through some pretty cold-assed winters without her hot little body next to me. She promised that she would be right there waiting for me. Only time will tell. But, I did tell her that if anything ever happened to me, she should move on to make a happy life for herself."

Allan was amazed. "You gave her permission?"

"Yes, I did. I hope that selfless act doesn't come back to bite me."

Tony closed his eyes and imagined this extraordinary opportunity to have that the life he had dreamed of for so long. It was only hours away now. His thoughts raced back to the last evening that he and Ruth had spent at the juke joint, topping it with greeting the sunrise in the hayloft. He replayed the visions, with the lingering effects that followed their roll in the hay. It was his vivid replication of life with her that kept the dream alive. To him, it had never diminished, regardless of the many years that had passed.

Allan was a little more optimistic. It had been only ten years since he left.

"Donna and I spent all our school years together and never imagined a future with someone else. We lived for each other, wanting nothing but a future together, regardless of what may happen. I imagine she still hasn't come up for air since I went away. It was a bonehead move to run off to war, but when they hit the twin towers, it was way too close to the farm. We were only seventy miles away. After we went to see the devastation, I felt that there was no other choice but to enlist."

Allan had argued with himself through the years that followed, that if she had found someone new, he would be able to forgive her. It was an argument that he lost most of the time. He was convinced that they were that tight. If she hadn't married when he returned, then he would win her back. The conflict stirred constantly in Allan's gut. His approach to deal with the strain of wondering was to poke others, just as he had on the night that he had met Pete and Frankie.

Allan deflected his own seriousness. "And you, Major Wood. What's in store for you?"

"Not sure. You all are living the stuff that movies are made of. I prefer not to talk about it."

Charlie declared. "There is nothing that bad. Didn't you have two kids? Just think of the excitement for them to see you again."

"I don't think so."

Ricky recalled the year leading up to his departure, and that day when he had made a low approach into a ball of fire. He had punished his family with his distracted manner for over a year. He had pushed his wife and children away, without shame. He had remained so focused on the war, the news, and all the negativity that had commanded his life then. He remembered the specific evening before he shipped out when he had ignored his children. He had been quite aware that they hungered and begged for his attention. It had been hateful on his part to do that to them, especially to Betty, who always held it together. He had expected at any time that they would leave because his behavior was so detestable. He had only begun to face his disgraceful ways after his death. It had taken such a horrific tragedy for him to change his perspective and accept that he was wrong.

He continued. "I was such a selfish bastard. I didn't care about myself after that, and I carried incredible remorse for my actions. I wouldn't blame them if they hated me. I deserved it. How could I hurt them so badly? They loved me unconditionally, and Betty had the patience of an angel. Charlie and Lesa were the victims of my horrible self-pity."

"I remember a time that Betty and I were so much in love, with not a worry in the world. We used to dance and party with our families and prayed that it would never end. I could tell you about her every move on the floor, her favorite song and how natural it was to complement each other's movements. We had so much happiness in our lives that we wanted others to share it with, so we had Lesa and Charlie. It couldn't have been any better than that."

Charlie argued. "They will remember the good times over the bad. It will be fine, Rick."

Tony added. "You should at least tell them how you feel and apologize. Sounds like they deserve an explanation."

Ricky conceded. "Yes, that's the least they deserve."

He thanked them for their words of support, and then they each went off to their markers for the evening. The night was still, and the moon hung high, casting shadows across the fields. The four spent their evening alone in peace, pondering the outcome of their return to their families. They greatly appreciated the second chance at life that others never got. Ultimately, they wanted to choose wisely this time to bring peace to themselves and their families. They thanked the stars for Pete's role in making it all happen.

PEARL

It was late in the evening when Charlie returned to Pearl Harbor. He chose not to go home. He thought it was all for naught because of the years that had passed. He looked at the reflection of the *Arizona* sitting alone with all the spirits within. At least he would have stories to share with his friends below. He caught a liberty launch that was taking a fallen *USS Arizona* Veteran for a burial within the hallowed walls of the massive metal tomb.

The Navy divers were ordered to deliver a deceased shipmate to his friends who waited below. Charlie's first thought was that it would be a new friend he would make aboard ship. He followed the burial detail onboard the memorial. Charlie remained back by the placards while the divers carried the remains below. He sat in the corner of the memorial and hung his head in defeat. To him, he had failed on so many counts, and then to ignore his gift to go home was that remaining rivet to his eternal coffin.

Charlie patiently waited for them to finish. He knew that once he went down again, it would be forever. They retired their shipmate below and shoved back off toward the pier. He would apologize profusely to the spirits for not going home, which he felt was letting everyone down. He remembered a time when he had been the strong one who gave hope to others.

"Charlie?"

He looked to see the origin of the voice. From around the corner walked a shadow, followed by an elderly woman.

He asked. "Do I know you? Mom?"

Charlie's heart jumped to his throat. After all these years his mom was right there. It's what he had hoped for with all of his might.

"No. It's me, Helen."

She moved into the light for him to see.

"Sis? Really?"

She chuckled. "Yes, your little sister all grown up and out."

They met with an embrace that filled seventy years of emptiness. Charlie broke down and sobbed uncontrollably. He had pent up emotions that he had never allowed to penetrate his dense armor. Holding his sister, Helen, let him free his internal demons of unbelievable sorrow.

He cried as he spoke. "I'm so sorry for leaving you the pain of my life."

She encouraged him to sit and catch his breath. She also needed the rest. Helen didn't want to cause him any more pain, but he nagged her to tell him the absolute truth.

"You never came back. That's what they couldn't wrap their minds around. To them, you drowned here every day for the last seven decades, or until they passed away. I was never successful in comforting them. Everything changed the day you died, but my life remained the same until I got the call to meet you here today."

"From whom?"

"I don't know. Someone. I thought I heard him say JFK?"

Charlie chuckled. He regained some levity knowing that the others at Arlington had known what his intentions were all along.

Charlie smiled. "Sis, you look great."

"Not as well-kept as you, Charlie."

They hugged, stepped back, and held hands. Charlie realized that not everyone would have a dreamy ending to his return home. However, he was quite content that he saw his sister and believed in his heart that his mother and father were somehow right there with them. Without question, they agreed that they would never pass up a chance like this again. He had gotten the closure he wanted and knew that now his sister would feel the same. He was sorry but thankful that she had given up real happiness to help their parents through the struggle.

Helen asked, "How did you end up here?"

"I was part of a young man's dream."

He didn't explain except to tell her that he had learned that a person should find someone to love, give that person his or her unconditional commitment, and never stop loving that person until it's time to go.

AGELESS

It was the early evening in Great Falls, Montana, when the bus pulled into town. It was much different than Tony had remembered. The roads had been paved and were much wider, which reduced the yards to a size that barely accommodated the front porches. A slight breeze was stirring that evening, and the sun rested on the horizon, giving a chill to the air.

Tony stepped down, took a deep breath and surveyed the neighborhood that he had left seventy years earlier. He decided to go to Ruth's parents' house since that was the last place that he had seen her. He resigned himself to the possibility that she wouldn't be there. Her absence would be accounted for that in that she had either died or found another. Even if she were there, she would be sixty-nine years older than he.

The bus driver asked if he had any gear below in the hold. Tony ignored the question and rushed out. He had just one thought in his head, to find Ruthie, and that could happen just minutes down the road. As he walked at a rapid pace, he was reminded of the great times that he and Ruth had had in the honky tonk that was now sporting an artsy façade. He wondered what the current appeal was, but more so why it would ever close? He hadn't had a chance to catch up to the technology and didn't quite understand the glass moving picture in the window, or how it worked.

Ruth's parents' house was about a half mile from the bus station. At his current pace, he would be there in five minutes. From a distance he saw an attractive elderly woman rocking slowly in a chair on the porch. Her silver hair was swept into a bun style and held neatly in place with a silver clip. Her cheeks mirrored the rouge color that lined her aged lips, and a flowery dress with a lace collar decorated her frail frame. She sat on an old, wooden rocker that faced town. As Tony got closer, he could hear her singing in a weak voice, "End of the World" by Skeeter Davis. He was unfamiliar with the tune, but it sounded quite sad.

As she rocked, she would think about him, and the years that had passed. She had never given up hope that someday she would see him again. For the better part of her life, she had worked as a nurse for the local hospital. Her outlet from heartache was to heal others, which she had done until she reached the age of seventy. She had mended others in hopes that someone would be there to mend Tony if he ever needed it. He had never returned from foreign soil, which gave her the hope that one day he would come back.

Tony was about twenty yards away, when he slowed his pace, with reservation. Ruth squinted to see the end of the street, watching the figure getting bigger as it approached. As he came closer, she grabbed her chest thinking that it was the end. She had often prayed to leave this world with her lifetime love standing before her. The figure walked like her fella. She looked over her glasses and blinked her eyes in an effort to clear her vision.

Tony yelled. "You kept your word!"

Now she could see a boy in uniform coming closer. She couldn't quite make out what he was saying.

He repeated himself. "You're right here, just as you promised."

Now the voice was becoming more familiar to her. Was it someone whom she had aided as a nurse?

"Ruthie, it's me!"

Now she was concerned. She thought that her wishes had come true, that she had died, and Tony was here to take her away to eternity together.

She remarked. "It's happening."

He slowed more with only feet to go. "What are you talking about?"

"It's over now."

"Hey, it's me, Tony."

She pinched herself because it was getting all too real.

He looked, walked, and talked like her lover.

With disbelief she asked, "Tony?"

"In the flesh, my love."

"Yes, and much younger than mine," she answered.

With each step that Tony took bringing him closer to Ruth, her body began to transform. The lines in her face began to fade, her hair filled with color, her smile became firm, and her once big brown eyes grew wide and began to sparkle with youth. She was impervious to her transformation because she was affixed to his image coming toward her.

She began to speak in a younger voice. "I told you that I'd love you for life. I kept my promise. I am here."

He stopped to marvel at the miracle before him. He was so full of life now that it was pouring out of his eyes, wetting the front of his shirt. He wanted this feeling to last until the twelfth of never. Everything that he had ever felt was there, encapsulated in that one moment. It was the incredible power of desire and fulfilled hope flowing between their bodies.

They couldn't wait another second. They met on the top stair in their youthful bodies of many years ago, with an embrace to last forever and ever. He held the fullness of her youthful figure so tightly, but she didn't mind.

He glowed passionately, as he had when they were teens. "Wow, baby."

"How did you . . . ? And how is this possible?"

He cut her off. "Sweetheart, it's a real long story, and I am going to take forever to tell you all about it, every detail."

They fell through the screen door and made their way back to the summer of 44.

Silence became the front porch, but within, you could hear the dropping of shoes and laughter going down the hallway.

Ruth had learned a lesson in seventy years of being alone. It was that commitment comes in two ways, voluntary and involuntary. She had chosen the first and had been rewarded with happiness. Late into the night, you could hear Ruthie singing Patsy Cline's "Walking after Midnight" to Tony. It had become her battle hymn of hope.

TEMPTATIONS

Ricky stood in his Dress Blues at the bar waiting for his chance to talk to Betty. He was anxious and apprehensive as to what the outcome might be. She was seated with her husband in the restaurant that adjoined the bar. He hadn't worked up the nerve to confront her, and he didn't have a plan of action yet. As he sipped his beer, he noticed two families make their way to her table. It was Lesa and Charlie, and their children. He smiled to think that these might be his grandchildren.

In a matter of minutes, the group was talking and laughing. The kids were occupied, deciphering the puzzles that they had gotten from the hostess. It was obvious that everyone was enjoying each other's company. Ricky began to wonder why he had ever come back. Betty appeared to be happy with this new guy. Ricky noticed that Lesa had many of the pretty facial features and the same attractive shape that Betty had had when she was young. He could tell from looking at Betty that the years had been kind to her. She was still a stunner today, just as she had once been when they first met. Charlie had grown into what Ricky saw as a sturdy, handsome gentleman. Ricky watched as Charlie and Lesa doted on their children. He immediately felt that they had gotten their good mannerisms from their mother. He wished that he had shown them that he was uncritically fond of them when they were young, so that they might have thought better of him now. He was looking for one thing, just one thing that he could see that was evidence that he had ever been part of that family.

Ricky was sitting on the end of the bar, facing the lengthy mirror, while he discretely watched his family's reflections as they interacted with each other. He got scared and turned his face away from Betty as he watched her coming toward him. She brushed by him on the way to the ladies room. She inquisitively slowed for a second look as she entered the restroom. He became concerned that she hadn't even recognized him, and now that he had a couple of minutes to think, his fear grew that they wouldn't know him even if he bit them.

He was grumbling on when he watched one child make his way to the hostess station for another puzzle. Ricky returned his attention to the ladies room door. He wasn't going to miss another opportunity to talk to Betty, away from the others. He was growing impatient, and then he felt a tug at his jacket.

"Mr., are you a pilot?"

He looked down. "Yes, I am."

My grandpa was a pilot. He looked like you. What's your name, Mr.?"

"My name is Ricky."

The little boy looked up and smiled. "Mine, too."

Ricky went weak in the knees. He was overcome by the exchange and the possibility that this little well-behaved young man was probably his grandson. Then it hit him like a ton of bricks; one of his children had named his or her boy after him. At this point, he was overflowing with emotion but knew that he would have to hold it together if he were going to talk to Betty.

Little Ricky smiled and shook his grandfather's hand.

"It was a pleasure meeting you, Mr."

Little Ricky scurried off to the table to deliver the paper to his sister, and then walked over to Betty, who had made it back to her seat undetected. The child put his arm around his grandmother's neck and whispered.

"Grandma, there's a pilot over there who looks just like Grandpa, and his name is Ricky, just like mine."

Betty whirled around to see who he was talking about. She recalled that familiar figure in the bar. Ricky had already postured himself out of her line of sight. He still didn't have a plan, and was too afraid to move into her view.

Her mind immediately drifted back to a time with Ricky, when they were happy and carefree. She couldn't explain it but felt compelled to wander the area, migrating to the bar where earlier she had seen that familiar shadow. She saw a can of Schaeffer at the end of the bar where the stranger had been sitting. It seemed eerie that it was Ricky's beer of choice.

The force pulled her to that spot, at which point she picked up the beer and held it in her hand. Ricky was watching in disbelief that she would make that association from so many years ago. She sat on that stool and stared off in the distance. She had become disengaged from her family now and was on another unconscious spiritual mission.

She began to wander around the restaurant in search of something that she couldn't explain. Her table was engrossed in conversation and activity so that she was never missed. A lonely jukebox's animated lights illuminated a lonely corner of the bar. Ricky was fascinated, watching her move about, and he remembered every attribute and action that became this woman whom he had loved so much, so long ago. His heart was beating incredibly fast as he moved closer to almost touch her. She definitely wasn't in the present with her sexy and youthful actions. As she leaned against the juke, he could predict her every movement as if he were her puppeteer.

He spoke lowly but with great exuberance.

"Okay, Betty . . . cross your legs, lean on your right elbow, run your finger up and down the selections till you find the mood, drop the coins in, and hit the keys simultaneously. Yep, you're right on track, Sweetheart."

He smiled throughout the entire performance.

Again, he foretold each measure of her dance.

His excitement soared. "Now the music begins. Step back, turn completely around, do that goofy mashed potato thing you do, and shuffle your feet."

He watched the glow in her eyes.

"Yes, that's it, Baby."

He was so focused on her moves that he didn't notice that she had played their favorite Four Tops song, "When She Was My Girl."

What happened next would be his salvation. Betty turned, looked up, pointed to the sky, winked, and blew a kiss.

It was in that single moment of unbelievable joy that Ricky knew that she still loved him. He stood speechless, so full of peace and love in his heart that he understood why he had been called here. He saw the happiness that had always been there, even during the tough times, and it still remained. She had been his angel all along, and as such, he needed to respect her strength and her decisions. With that, he decided not to interrupt the new life that his family had chosen, but the thing that meant more to him than anything else was that they had forgiven him years ago.

He took one long look at what he had created such a long time ago, tipped his hat to their table, and walked out the door with the song still in his heart.

SACRIFICES

Donna sat on the bleachers in Times Square. She had taken the day off to visit the newly opened 911 Memorial. Her thoughts were with Allan and their life together that had been lost. She wondered where she would have been today had he not gone to fight. It had been eight years since he left her, but she still hadn't left him.

Donna's intentions were to take this day to make a decision in her life that makes it more productive and happy. It was something that she had been unable to do, regardless of the urging of friends and family for her to move on. She somehow needed to hear it from Allan. No matter how many private sessions she had held with his spiritual audience, it always left her empty and unwilling to go forward.

Time very quickly slipped away that morning. She had planned a lunch date with Stephen to tell him that she was ready to move forward, however, her attempt to come to closure this morning had again been unsuccessful. Stephen originated from Boston and clearly was at home in the big city. They had met while jogging in Central Park. His business career had just begun, and his future was filled with promise. He was clearly at the opposite end of the lifestyle spectrum than the one she and Allan had shared, but he had a great heart and loved her passionately just the same.

Her emotions were all over the chart this morning. The only thing that she was consistent with in her life was putting Stephen second to her memories. Donna had taken a job in New York City for a change of scenery. She had hoped that a new location, unfamiliar to her past, would move her forward in life.

Allan stepped up the bleachers to be close to her. He could see that she had been crying and wanted so badly to hold her. He remained in spirit to gain an edge on her psyche. He saw a young, professionally dressed man walk up and sit on the other side of her.

"Hey, Donna."

"Hi."

She asked, "So, how long will you be gone?"

"I'm not really sure. It depends on what you tell me."

The ball was in her court, and all she could do was fumble.

"I'm sorry, Stephen."

"So, we are on hold again?"

"I need more time to sort it out."

"Donna, you have had almost ten years. Why can't you get past this?"

"I don't know."

Allan knew her well enough to see that she was breaking inside. Her eyes were empty, her actions lethargic, and her once incredible spirit, diminished. He was at a disadvantage now to break into the conversation. He sat helplessly as they continued.

Stephen asked, "Are you still thinking about him?"

She barked. "His name is Allan!"

Stephen sat silently after he heard the name. He thought about the scene from Gone with the Wind when Rhett wanted to squeeze Ashley out of Scarlett's memory. He felt that he was losing steam in this relationship, and he decided to make his proclamation.

"Donna, you know that I love you from the sky and back and that I would do anything for you, but I can't keep this up. I won't be back until you have made room in your life for me. I didn't bring any past into this romance so that it would be fresh and vibrant. However, you keep plaguing it with a memory of something that will never be. He is always in our company, always. I've only allowed this to go on this long out of respect for a man who gave so much to others. You are just punishing yourself for something that you didn't do."

"Steve, I'm so sorry. I want more, but something won't let me."

Stephen got up and took two steps down.

Donna offered a plea. "Please don't be mad."

"I'm not mad; frustrated is more like it. You're frozen in time, and the warmest love that I give to you won't thaw your cold, cold heart."

Allan moved a little closer, like he was going to protect her from Stephen's unkind words, but no one could see that. He watched her body language to validate her feelings with every word that Stephen spoke. He never imagined returning as this helpless spirit, when all he wanted to do now was to console her.

Her next words would capture Allan's attention.

"I wish that someone could help me."

"Lindz, that's exactly what I'm trying to do, but you won't let me."

Stephen stepped back up and tenderly kissed her on the forehead. "I'm sorry, Sweetheart. Please call me when we can be just us."

He walked down the stairs and into the crowd. Donna bowed her head and became numb to everything around her. She wanted to think about it but couldn't. He was right. She was frozen and unable to move on. Allan could see that she loved Stephen, but she just wouldn't shake the memory of her and Allan before he went to war.

It became clear what he should do when he saw her pain. Allan didn't want to transition out of spirit for fear that she would never heal. He moved closer for her to feel his effect. She tried very hard to dig out of this hole she had been for the years that Allan had been gone.

She sensed a presence, and, as she had so many times before, she talked to it.

"Allan, I really don't need this now. I was just beginning to cross the threshold of wanting to move on. We can't resurrect what we had, and at this point I don't know that I would want to. I've worked myself past a life that was unreal. I've lost ten years of my life continuing to live with this ghost that is just that, a ghost. Please leave me alone and let me go. Stephen is a great guy and has put up with my crap; I mean our crap, for too long. He doesn't deserve it. Please let me go."

Allan fell back to the seat behind. He was blown away by her emotion, but he realized that this was emotion that she had carried in his favor for almost a decade. He knew that it wasn't fair to her, and he knew that no matter what he did or said, it would never be the same pure innocence that they had explored so many years ago. It took him less than a New York minute to know what was right for her. He also realized that he wasn't being fair to himself, because he hadn't moved on, either. That concept sounded strange to him, however, he had never really let go either to allow her to go on.

He began to free her from her self-built prison with his words.

"Jess, I never wanted to hurt you or make you unhappy, but somehow I accomplished both. You are the last person, ever, that I would want to keep from lifelong happiness. For the last ten years, all I have dreamed of is walking through the fields, floating down the Delaware, and playing with our children until death do us part. I just forgot that we did part, and it was death that made it a reality. The dream was real to me, and it seems like you were dreaming the same dream. Well, this is not a dream for you. It is reality, and you have to get with it kid. You gave your life to me, even after I was gone. It's time that you give yourself life."

Allan felt that she had heard his plea because she smiled and began to speak.

"Allan, I loved you with all my heart and never wavered that you would come home to help me. I feel that you are here, sitting next to me. It's the greatest feeling that I've had in a long, long time, but I can't continue this way. If I don't let go and grab this golden opportunity, that somehow I feel you sent me, then I am an idiot and don't deserve it. I only hope that I can convince him that you are in my past, and that I won't pack you in my baggage anymore."

Allan thought that he would be angry, but actually he was relieved that he had probably performed his most unselfish act, ever. He smiled with one lonely tear that made its way to his heart.

He stood up, smiled, and had one last request. "Can I have a hug?"

Donna stood reaching out to space to cradle a spirit that would forever be only that to her. "I love you, Allan."

She wrapped her arms around her torso in what would be her final farewell to someone who would always have a special place in her heart. People in the street watched this young woman wrapped in happiness and hope, and they sighed. They knew that the angels had just saved another soul.

JOURNEY THROUGH TIME

The last time that had Pete walked through the gates of Arlington, his mood had been gloomy. This day would be much better than the last when he had come to bury his friend and comfort his friend's widow and son. He had just ingratiated himself with the most important person in his life, and now was about to visit his real father's grave for the first time in his adult life. Pete had a certain bounce in his step, and a smile that would effortlessly carry him there.

He had lain awake for most of the night before, crafting a real future for himself, and now he was about to stand before his father's grave to share his past, present, and future. In the span of just a couple of weeks, Pete had learned about mutual trust, confidence, and respect, accepting those who were worthy without condition. It was imperative that to further his own peace, he would need to be open and honest with others, and himself.

He arrived and was directed to the upper parking area to the left of the entrance. He had the advantage to sit for a bit and watch the people flow in. There were young, uniformed soldiers there with their families, each in their own minds beginning the training of what to expect if they went to war. Some wanted to be the highly decorated hero who saved the platoon, while others were exploring the possibility of being carried through the gates.

Pete understood both trains of thought, but had learned that neither appealed to him. He wanted to do his part without the fanfare. He had seen the aftermath for those left behind. He thought about his dream, and the four young men who would have gone home. How would it have turned out for them if it were true? He tried to sort out the events of the funeral and the familiarity that went with it. Those thoughts would have to wait for another day. Right now, his mission was to visit his father.

The pathway from the parking lot led to a hallway that further directed him to the right, where he came to an information counter. He anxiously waited his turn behind two other people. Pete looked at the worker's name tag and smiled.

"Good afternoon, Gladys. I'm looking for a marker. It would have been from 1988, U.S. Navy."

"Sir, do you have a name?"

"Yes Ma'am. Petty Officer First Class Andrew Brucher."

Gladys could see that he was nervous. It was the first time that Pete had publicly used his father's name. It seemed so foreign to say it. She excused herself and then emerged with the coordinates scratched on a piece of paper.

"You will find him at section 27, marker 2649. You seem pretty excited."

Pete smiled. "I am."

"If you don't mind my asking, who is it that you are visiting?"

"I will see my dad for the first time in twenty two years. Thank you."

Before she could speak, he was out the door, heading towards the cemetery. In his haste, he had forgotten a map. He was almost ready to turn around and go back when a soldier approached him.

"Hey Sailor, you will probably need this."

Pete thought it odd that someone would have the wherewithal to know that he needed a map. He took it, thanked him, and headed out. He was preoccupied with finding the marker, and not interested in somebody's intuition. He unfolded the map and began matching the numbers to the coordinates.

He talked to himself as he walked.

"Let's see, I have to head this way to the newer section. Damn, there is a lot of ground to cover. Where's a good ghost when you need him? I sure could use those crazy-assed vets this afternoon. They had this place suit cased. "I'm sure my daddy knows everyone here. Yeah, why isn't he here to greet me? Instead, I'm hunting for him. Doesn't he care enough to greet me?"

He laughed at his creativity and continued the search. Ten minutes later, Pete passed by Audie Murphy's grave. It was covered with rocks, coins, flowers, patches, and photos. Murphy's cairn served as the temple for all warriors, from WWII vets to present day combatants. Pete sustained his brisk pace toward section 27. As he neared, he coached himself aloud. "Okay, down this row. Here's marker 2601. Fifty more to go."

He saw a person sitting on a marker at the far end. As he got closer, he noticed that it was a young boy dressed in an old style army uniform. Pete ignored him and counted the numbers. The nearer he walked, the greater his curiosity became. Finally, he reached the boy. He looked behind the marker to see 2649. Then he walked around and nudged the boy out of the way so he could read the name. Engraved in the stone was "Buck." Pete became agitated.

"Who are you? This is supposed to be Andrew Brucher's grave."

Buck pointed to the marker. "I'm Buck, Pete."

"Why are you here, and how the hell do you know my name?"

"This is my spot, and I've known about you for twenty years."

Pete shook his head in confusion. He looked at the coordinates that were on the paper, and then at the map. Buck stood and smiled.

"I'm going back to get the right directions."

Buck quickly responded. "You have them."

Pete snapped. "Like I told you, I'm looking for Andrew Brucher."

Buck grinned. "I know, and that's why I'm here."

Pete wagged his finger. "Listen little man. I'm not in the mood for games."

Buck motioned for Pete to follow him. "C'mon Pete. I'll take you to him."

Pete could see that Buck was uneducated and limited on social skills. He quickly realized that he wasn't going to make him understand the seriousness of his quest, so he followed for a few minutes.

Pete stopped and grabbed Buck out of frustration.

"Where are we going, and how do you know my father?"

Buck pulled forward in the same direction, while answering his questions.

"I've been here since1917. I was killed in World War I and buried here a little after that. I never talked to anybody until I met Andrew after he died about twenty years ago. He asked me to be his friend."

Buck continued his story of loneliness and how Pete's father had changed that for him. Andrew had shared stories with Buck about his life with Arlene and Pete, and the love that their family had. He had shared his hardships and regrets and given Buck an identity and belongingness that he'd never known.

It seemed so bizarre that this kid, of maybe fourteen years, knew Pete's dad so much better than he did. As they walked, Buck told Pete about this incredible closeness and love that he had found with another human being. He told Pete that he had started his life with no one and no place to call home, and then his life had ended almost instantaneously when he blindly followed others into war, not even understanding who was fighting, and why. He finished by telling him that ultimately he had died for something he didn't understand.

Buck exuded a freshness of spirit and hope that was indescribable, and it was from a person who had been thrown out, tossed around, and then terminated by others, who had never come to know him. Pete learned that the greatness of a man, his father, had saved this soul from total despair. He thought to himself that Andrew Brucher was a pretty special man. Pete had grown mighty proud in the past thirty minutes, from what had merely begun as an act of human kindness by his father, influencing the spirit of this young boy. Pete became very anxious to meet this man.

FATHER FIGURE

They had covered the distance of a football field when Buck stopped. Pete looked ahead on the stone that faced them. It read, Sergeant Andrew Brucher, U.S. Army, July 4, 1988. He was focused on the name and the stone carving that articulated his father's information.

Buck interrupted Pete's attention. "I come here a lot. I pick him up, and we head over to the old amphitheater to listen to stories."

Pete cut his eyes at Buck. "Do you mind?"

"Sorry. Let me know when you're done."

"Can I please spend some time with him in private?"

Buck replied. "He's not here."

"He's not here? What are you talking about?"

Buck explained that he had met Andrew in the summer of 1991 and that he had been in bad shape. Andrew told Buck that he had lost his wife and son, and couldn't get back to them to apologize. Buck shared his life of nothing with Andrew, and for some reason, it lifted his spirit. Andrew said it was because he had had a taste of happiness with you and your mom and I had never even been offered the goblet.

Buck continued his story, saying that he and Andrew would share their pieces of life, and the tragedies that had befallen each of them. When Buck finished his stories, Andrew would rally with a heartfelt saga that brought laughter to their hearts. It seemed that each of them fed off the other to build a bond that was unbreakable. Buck would learn to love and would teach Andrew to be thankful for all that he had once had. Buck's inspiration had apparently changed Andrew and helped him to become happy.

Though Pete was touched by the musings, he wanted an answer. "So, where is Andrew?"

"I thought you knew."

"If I knew, I wouldn't be asking."

"Well, Allan, Tony, Charlie, Ricky, and I were the five recruited."

"Buck, I only picked four."

"Yup, then your dad asked Audie if I could be the fifth, and he agreed. I only had to carry Frankie's casket with the four and your dad, and then I could go back home to experience a life that I never knew."

Pete stood motionless, waiting.

Buck continued. "Well, I wanted to pay Andrew back for all he had done for me all those years, so I gave up my spot to Andrew so he could go back to see Arlene." There was nothing for me to see in New Orleans, and, well, you know. I needed to do it for my friend."

Pete, still confused, asked, "So, where is Andrew right now?"

"He said he was going to see Arlene."

Thoughts relentlessly streamed through Pete's head.

He finally found his voice. "Holy shit, when?"

Buck smiled. "Right after you left. He didn't want to intrude on your visit with her, so he waited until today. He's supposed to be back tonight. Andrew wanted me to ask you to stay until he returned."

Pete's first thoughts were that he should be there with his mom and dad, but he knew that couldn't be possible. Then, he began to wring his hands with worry about what was happening at the house this very minute.

"What if Kent comes home while Dad's there?"

"Don't worry Pete. It'll be fine. You know, the two were so much in love."

"That's why I'm troubled at the thought."

"So if they get together, what's wrong with that?"

"It wouldn't be fair to Kent."

"Your dad has been waiting a long time. This is a time for closure for him, a second chance. It's the two most important people in your life. Don't you want them to have closure? I never had a mother or father. It makes me bust wide open to know that I have finally given my love to someone. Andrew is the only father that I will ever know. I can't wait to hear about his visit tonight."

Pete sat on the grass, leaning forward, hugging his knees. He still couldn't believe it all. They remained quiet for the greater part of the hour. He had had no control over the outcomes of events over the last week, so why should he fight it now?

Buck jumped up. "Let's go! We're supposed to meet at Lee's house for the homecoming debriefs."

Homecoming Debriefs

The combination of exciting stories with a perfectly moonlit night made the evening inviting to all. You could feel the anticipation building as the resident spirits made their way toward General Lee's home. The sea of warriors flowed, filling the hillside with anxious fans of the special returning heroes of second chances. The guests of honor, Frankie, Tony, Allan, and Ricky had already taken their positions to talk. The only missing link was Andrew.

JFK and Audie sat to the side. At this point, Pete just went with it. He didn't concern himself with whether this was a dream again, or something else. He kept a vigilant watch for his dad to show. The debriefs turned to stories of family, love, character, and forgiveness. The four men had accomplished the greatest gift for themselves; it was that they had forgiven themselves. This was the most important act that had allowed them to bring closure to their lives.

They told of going home and their changes of heart after seeing their families. They understood the choices that their families had made and the dynamics that had been in effect after their deaths. Specifically, they took great pride in the knowledge that they had made a difference for those they had loved and lost. It warmed everyone's hearts when they realized that they, too, would have made similar choices.

Tony was the only one of the four who would be returning home to his past to live out his days. Pete kept scanning the crowd for the face in the picture that his mom had handed him earlier in the week. He grew concerned that something had happened. Or, was Andrew not coming back, having decided to stay with Arlene? The waning night wasn't giving him much hope. The crowds began to leave, until only a few remained.

Pete asked, "Buck, where is he?"

Buck shrugged his shoulders.

He had all but given up hope when he noticed two figures walking his way. As they got closer to the light, Pete heard a familiar voice. "Hey, Shipmate."

"Frankie?"

"Yep, in the flesh. Well, almost."

As Frankie came into the light, Pete noticed the person to his left. It took less than a second for Pete to realize that this young man was the spitting image of himself.

"Pete, sorry we're late. I waited for him at the front gate so I wouldn't miss the reunion."

Pete asked, "Dad?"

"Yes, Son. It's been too long."

They embraced to capture twenty-two lost years. Buck began to cry. His tears of joy flowed for the man who had become his father, big brother, his life. This moment was the highlight of Buck's life. Onlookers choked back the emotion. They wanted to capture this, forever. It would have to last them a lifetime.

The rest of the crowd dispersed. The only ones remaining were Buck, Frankie, Andrew, and Pete. Buck and Frankie kept their distance to offer Pete and Andrew time to catch up.

Pete smirked. "So Dad, how did the visit go with Mom?"

"That's personal, Son."

"Dad?"

"Seems strange that you call me Dad. We are the same age. Please call me Andy."

"Can't do it, Dad."

"Alright. First of all, everything went great. It was incredible seeing Arlene. I mean, Mom."

"Did you meet Kent?"

"No, that would have been awkward. I don't think he would have understood, or approved of the visit. I can't believe that I'd ever say it, but I admire all that he did for you and Mom. Until I saw her again, all I wanted to do was kick his ass, knowing that he was sleeping with her."

"What happened when she saw you?"

"Well, when I got to the house she was in the shower. Not really, I'm joking. I was so nervous. It was just like our first date. When I walked in, she was sitting in the kitchen listening to someone named Adele. The song was 'Someone Like You.'" It kind of fit the visit. I guess she found someone like me."

Andrew stood there smiling as he shared the reunion with Pete. Pete could see that his heart was breaking all over again. He could see the pain in his father's eyes that he wouldn't be spending life with her. He told Arlene that his visit back to her was a gift from Buck, a young boy who had nothing, but still had the most to give. He said that Buck had given him the opportunity to see that his family was okay.

Andrew was proud of the choices she had made, that although difficult, were the correct ones for everyone. She had been kind to herself, and that was all that Andrew ever wanted after he had gone. By Buck's unselfish gift, Andrew had been able to calm his restless heart. Andrew remarked in jest that it was the first time that Arlene had let him talk without interruption.

With that, Frankie interrupted. "Are you coming back? It's getting pretty late, and you can't go past curfew."

Pete looked at his dad. "Will I be able to come back to visit? You know, see you?"

"That's up to you, Son."

"What do you mean?"

"Alignment of the stars and . . ."

Pete poked Andrew. "Ha, funny."

Most of the cemetery residents had disappeared over the hill. The four remaining assembled to say goodnight. Buck told them that the two greatest gifts to this world were from Andrew, and one was Pete.

Pete asked, "What is the other, Buck?"

"He was the first person to ever tell me that he was glad that I was born."

Pete reached out and hugged him like his little newfound brother. Buck walked away with a smile on his face and a song in his heart. They were amazed and overjoyed with what could come out of total desperation.

Andrew faced Pete. "Well, Son, it's that time."

They didn't speak. Their embrace said it all. Andrew turned and abruptly left to hide his tears. He walked quickly to catch up to Buck.

Pete called to Andrew. "See you soon, Dad."

Frankie and Pete were the only ones still standing there.

Frankie offered, "I'll walk you to the gate, Shipmate. I want to thank you for taking care of Sara, Austin, and the folks. Most of all, for bringing us back. How did you ever call up the spirits? You, my friend, made the impossible possible. We all hoped that through our mistakes, your life lessons would be few. Because of you, there are thousands who won't continue to carry the weight of regret. You saved them from themselves. Essentially, your life has just begun with a measure of peace that many may never know. You were right, Pete. Life is all about choices."

They stood at the gate for a few minutes to take in the moment. Frankie hugged his friend.

"Pete, don't ever forget. You've been my brother and confidant, and you have traveled to the end with me.

Pete asked, "Frankie, will you do me one last favor?"

Frankie replied, "Name it, Brother."

"Take care of Dad and Buck?"

Frankie responded with tears, "Only if you'll look after Sara and Austin."

"Done."

They went their separate ways. Pete walked toward the parking lot with sunrise staring him in the face. He saw it as the symbol of his new day.

KEEPING WATCH

The flashlight shone brightly in Pete's face. It took several taps on the driver's window to awaken the sleeper. The light had barely illuminated the sleeping figure that lay across the front seat. The shadow from the Marines raising the flag had provided enough cover to let Pete sleep. He awakened enough to rummage the keys from the floorboard and insert the right one into the ignition. It took a tug on the wheel in order to free the steering lock and turn the key for power. First the back window began to lower, and then with further searching, he fumbled to open the driver's window.

Pete's raspy voice rang through. "Yes?"

The security guard answered. "It's going to be morning soon. I was concerned if you were alright. You've been zoned out all evening."

"How long?"

"Since 2300."

"Thanks Officer."

"Not a problem. I didn't have the heart to wake you. You looked so peaceful."

"I think I am now."

The guard smiled. "Have a good night, and drive safe."

"Officer, I want to thank you for taking care of these fine men who once took care of us. You are a real trooper."

"That I was . . . U.S. Army Trooper, 1st Cavalry Division, Iraq. I was one of the lucky ones who made it home to my family. After that, I pledged myself to take care of others who didn't make it back. Have a good night."

Pete smiled. "Thank you for your service to our country."

"It was my pleasure."

EPILOGUE

This story has been hiding within me for forty-seven years. Long ago, I lay awake in my room upstairs, eavesdropping on a conversation between Kenneth Just and my parents about his pending deployment to Vietnam. Kenneth was known to us as George, and he was probably about 22 years old at the time. On this particular night, his voice seemed a little more serious as he talked with my folks.

The war in Vietnam was becoming all too real, and it was really affecting the young men who helped their families work the farms during the day and chased their local high school sweethearts by night.

As a young school boy, I would try to emulate the upper classmen who were popular with the girls. It seemed that they were the elite ones, who held the world in their hands and would eventually command a life that would be free from the turbulence of war. I remember Allan Milk stealing kisses from his sweetheart, Donna, in the hallways of Delaware Valley Central, much to the chagrin of the teachers. Today, I smile at the memory of his bravery back then. He embraced every moment of life when he could. Little did any of us know that those kisses would have to hold him a lifetime and beyond. I'm sure she hasn't forgotten them either.

To us, war was just a word in a book with very little meaning. An older, red-headed teacher named Bertha shared the concept of war with us in World History class. The real lessons on war should have been given as testimonials by Korean War and World War II veterans who could teach us about real world expectations. I believe that every young man and woman should meet these gents to learn about strength and honor and devotion to family and country.

During the war in Vietnam, the draft brought a new reality to the young men in our area and stole the spirit of life. It transformed our concept of war into a cruel reality that only our fathers could articulate. Casualty numbers were a big part of the news every evening, adding to the anxiety of those who functioned in the unknown.

Then one day, out of the blue, news arrived that Allan Milk had been killed by a hand grenade. That's when the numbers became names. The very thought still moves me today. What about his family, his girl, and his dreams? This was a real person, whom we knew and loved.

This book is my way of apologizing to the many families who have been left behind without closure about the deaths of their loved ones. It is also a tribute to those who so gallantly gave, and in so many ways, continue to give to their country. I've never forgotten their names and have the deepest respect for the sacrifices that were gifted by them to this nation. Although we may never all agree on the purpose of war, we can all come together to thank and honor those who have given their lives, even if it was for a four-year enlistment.

I awoke early one morning with Ricky, Allan, Andy, Charlie, Tony, Pete, and Frankie on my mind. I couldn't escape my thoughts except by writing down the recurring pain. I wanted to thank them publicly again for their time and sacrifice for all of us. I consider each and every one of them as an incredible human being. My 28 years that I served in the Navy pale in comparison to any infantryman who ever had to walk into the line of fire. I at least was able to convey that to Tony every chance I got. He was my greatest personal hero by his contribution of gallantry on the field, and his equaled bravery when he faced the pain of Agent Orange up until the day he left our world to meet up with Pete, Charlie, Ricky, Allan, Andrew, and last but not least the love of his life, my sister, Ruth Ann. It was so important to me to tout his unquestionable guts and integrity to his face while he was here.

These men bravely fought for this nation, and they did it for people whom they would never even meet, people who walk among us today. Although many of these fine young men are no longer with us physically, I believe that they walk among us today, watching their families, and guiding them in their daily thoughts and actions. I believe that it's one soldier's strength of spirit that carries his mother to his marker every Memorial Day to memorialize his life.

Recently, I spoke on the phone with a hero's mother, who religiously attends memorials to mourn the loss of her son, who was taken away from her almost fifty years ago. From others' accounts, it's heart wrenching to watch her struggle to his grave to talk to him spiritually. We will never know the pain that she carries inside. During a recent conversation, she asked me if I could understand her pain, but all I could do was to fall silent with tears that she would not see. I am sorry for the burden that was left to her. I am so proud of the soldier's legacy and feel deep inside that his pride of her strength and his love for her has never diminished.

I also had the extreme pleasure of talking with Ricky Wood's brother. He talked about getting a letter from Ricky the day after Ricky was killed. He read it once and then put it away. Some things in life are just that difficult.

I spoke to a surviving hero yesterday about his life today. He is another casualty of the war in Vietnam. Although he didn't fall from a bullet, he is slowly dying a more painful death from the evils of Agent Orange. He is an incredible hero, who loved his comrades and has felt their losses his entire life. He thinks about them every day. He shared a story about himself and his comrades with me yesterday.

Their journey began when Les Burr drove his son, Tony, and Allan, Andy, Ricky, Frankie, Charlie, and Earl to Penn Station in New York City. The train then took them to Ft. Jackson, SC, with a subsequent flight to Ft. Carson, CO, for basic training. Subsequent flights would be to Vietnam. Only three of those brave young men would make it back before the war ended. Of those three, Tony passed away a few years ago from the effects of Agent Orange. Frankie is a victim of Agent Orange, and keeps the memories of those friends before him, and then his day will come to sit with the others to discuss their days of hunting, farming and chasing high school sweethearts.

Pete Baker was a U.S. Marine who fought on Okinawa. He carried horrific images of his tours of duty throughout his entire life. His memories of war consumed many of the 42 years of his marriage. He was only able to forget the tragedy and pain of war when he came home to the loss of his five-year-old son, who tragically lost his life. It was certainly a trade that he never wanted to make.

Today's warriors come back to us in many ways. Some are carried home, some come home with prosthetic limbs, and some arrive with the hidden injury of Post-Traumatic Stress Syndrome. Regardless, they have all served honorably and without regard to their own wellbeing, but with the intention of protecting their families and this nation. We owe each and every one of them an incredible debt of gratitude for their sacrifices now and forever.

I strongly feel that all heroes deserve our belief that they will always be here, guiding us, watching us, and believing that we will never forget who they are. That single act alone will ensure that their choices were not in vain.

The characters that these fine gents portrayed were merely to remind us of the names of those heroes. In real life each and every one of them was the epitome of honesty, goodness, and love. They were, in real life, courageous and exuded all of those honorable and admirable attributes that made them the finest of men. They were the best of the best in the world.

When you look at their photographs you will see real men whom we should remember each and every day in the freedoms that we enjoy in the United States of America. They each carried a pride that ran to their very core. From all accounts of family and friends these fine, spirited gentlemen were the elite of humanity. It was all because of them and their priceless gift to all of us that keeps them in our hearts, minds, and prayers. May they forever be free of a *restless heart.*

SP4 Richard Alan Wood, United States Army, Vietnam

SP4 Allan Arlyn Milk, United States Army, Vietnam

Sgt. Andrew Brucher

Sergeant Andrew Carl Brucher, United States Army, Vietnam

SP4 Leslie Anthony Burr, United States Army, Vietnam

Corporal Peter Baker, United States Marine Corps, WWII

Petty Officer Second Class Charles Ernest Koberlein
United States Navy, Vietnam

SP4 Frank Leonardo, United States Army, Vietnam

Buck

In Remembrance of all Soldiers, with a Multitude of thanks for their Courage, Service, and Dedication to our Country and for Freedom. Rest well and know that you will NEVER BE FORGOTTEN . . . .

"NOW ARISES FROM HALLOWED GROUND A DELICATE CLOUD OF BUGLE NOTES THAT SOFTLY SAY, GO TO SLEEP . . . . COMRADES TRUE, BORN ANEW, PEACE TO YOU. YOUR SOULS SHALL BE WHERE THE HEROES ARE AND YOUR MEMORIES SHINE LIKE THE MORNING STAR . . . . SLUMBER WELL, WHERE THE SHELLS SCREAMED AND FELL . . . . THE DANGER HAS PASSED, AND NOW AT LAST, GO TO SLEEP" . . . . By ~ Sgt Joyce Kilmer, 165th US Infantry (formerly 69th NYNG) KIA Ourcq, France~July 30, 1918 ~To the Everlasting Glory of The Infantry~

Acknowledgements

General Lawrence Snowden, U.S. Marines, WWII, Korea, Vietnam
Rear Admiral Stephen Keith, U.S. Navy (ret) Cover Art
Lesa Wood, Copy Editor
Heather Whitaker, Content Editor

Service Organizations for their Continued Veteran Support:

Veterans of Foreign Wars
American Legion
Wounded Warriors
Prisoners of War / Missing in Action
Paralyzed Veterans of America
Vietnam Veterans of America
Korean War Veterans of America
WWII War Veterans of America
United Services Organization
Homes for Our Troops
AMVETS
Disabled Veterans
MOAA
Fisher House Foundation
Rolling Thunder
Mid-Eastern United States Memorial Wall
Student Veterans of America

Made in the USA
San Bernardino, CA
23 February 2014